CONNECT THE DOTS
MAKING SENSE OF THE BIBLE

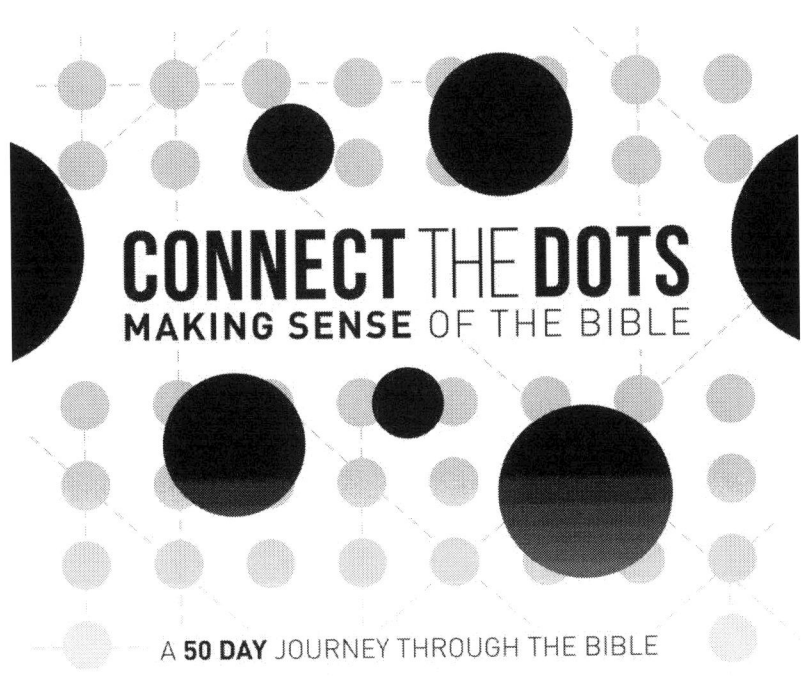

CONNECT THE DOTS
MAKING SENSE OF THE BIBLE

A **50 DAY** JOURNEY THROUGH THE BIBLE

WRITTEN BY:
RON COONEY
WITH
DEBORAH JENSEN

Visit Calvary Church at **www.Calvary.us**

© 2014 Calvary Church, Clearwater, FL

All rights reserved. No more than 250 words of this document may be reproduced, stored in a retrieval system, or transmitted in any form or by any means, electronic, mechanical, photocopying, recording, or otherwise, without the prior permission of the author.

Scripture quotations are from the *Holy Bible, New King James Version* unless otherwise noted. Copyright ©1982 by Thomas Nelson, Inc. Used by permission. All rights reserved.

Scripture quotations marked NIV are taken from the *Holy Bible, New International Version*, NIV® Copyright ©1973, 1978, 1984, 2011 by Biblica, Inc.™ Used by permission. All rights reserved worldwide.

Scripture quotations marked NLT are taken from the *Holy Bible, New Living Translation*. Copyright ©1996, 2004. Used by permission of Tyndale House Publishers, Inc., Wheaton, Illinois. All rights reserved.

Scripture quotations marked ESV are taken from the *Holy Bible, English Standard Version*. Copyright © by Good News Publishers. Used by permission. All rights reserved.

Scripture taken from the NEW AMERICAN STANDARD BIBLE®, Copyright © 1960,1962,1963,1968,1971,1972,1973,1975,1977,1995 by The Lockman Foundation. Used by permission.

Scripture quotations marked HCSB are taken from the Holman Christian Standard Bible®, Copyright © 1999, 2000, 2002, 2003, 2009 by Holman Bible Publishers. Used by permission.

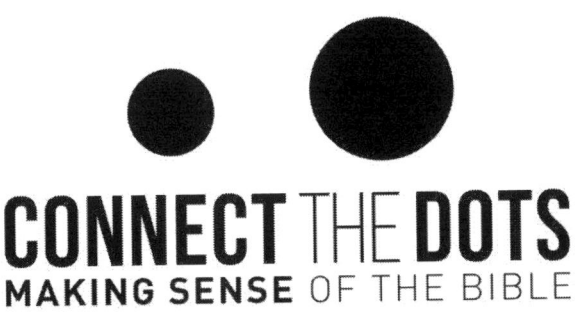

How to Use This Resource	6
Moms & Dads	8
The List: 50 Characters in the Bible	11
Bonus List: Twelve Facts About *The Dirty Dozen*	49
Old Testament Summary	65
New Testament Summary	107
50-Day Reading Plan	137
Timeline	173
Index List	177
Notes	194

How to Use This Resource

Most of us are familiar with the stories of Adam and Eve, Cain and Abel, Noah and the ark, Jacob and Esau, David and Goliath, and Jonah and the whale, among others. But do you know how these stories fit together to form a beautiful picture of the redemption of mankind?

The resources included in this book will help you connect the dots of the Bible-stories you know so well, giving you a comprehensive framework to understand the Bible. Use this book as you yield time to God each day in your personal quiet time, to help you prepare for a small group that you are a part of, and to use along with sermons that are preached to enrich your understanding of what is being taught.

The List

This section will give you a snapshot of fifty characters in the Bible and will aid you in your study of individuals in the Bible. Use the index on p. 178-179 to locate a person you need information on for a quick reference. You will also find other pages where this character is mentioned.

Bonus List

As a bonus, you will find *Twelve Facts About The Dirty Dozen*. These twelve evil characters in the Bible are a reminder of how important it is to take care in how you live. If you choose to live outside of God's love, you must live with the consequences of that decision. As you study, learn from these twelve characters what caused their downfall and how they reacted to God's corrective hand.

Books of the Bible Summary

Throughout history, God has recorded and preserved the Bible to help you better understand His character and divine plan for your life.

> *For everything that was written in the past was written to teach us, so that through the endurance taught in the Scriptures and the encouragement they provide we might have hope* (Romans 15:4, NIV).

The summaries of the books of the Bible provide you with a quick reference about key information concerning each book. Read about the authors of the book, important characters, dates, locations, and themes.

Use the book summaries to guide you in studying the books of the Bible or to refer to certain books when studying their authors. For instance, Jeremiah wrote the book of Jeremiah, but he also wrote the book of Lamentations. Paul authored almost half of the New Testament.

50-Day Reading Plan

Use the accompanying 50-Day Reading Plan to take in the Bible as a whole. As you read larger sections of scripture at one time – instead of a verse here and a verse there – you will begin connecting the dots in your mind about how the Bible fits together.

During the 50-Day Reading Plan, write the connections you make in this book or in your Bible to help you in the future. When you complete the 50 days, you can go back and study a person of interest or an account from the Bible that intrigued you the most.

Moms & Dads

If you have never taken the time to read the Bible to your children, this is a great way to start!

In addition to the 50-Day Reading Plan, we have included readings for you to use with your younger children based on the *Jesus Storybook Bible* written by Sally Lloyd-Jones. We recommend you read the appropriate day's entry and discuss the passage together as a family.

To stay on pace with your reading plan, we have included activities and review on certain days when there is no assigned scripture reading. This family devotion time can take five minutes or thirty minutes, depending on your family's unique situation.

Keep in Mind

Make God a part of your entire day, not just a portion of it. As you learn the bigger story of God, you will see how a sunset points to the beauty of God or how a bird, singing in the morning, is a reminder of how much God cares for you.

As you talk to your children about God in the details of life, you give them a framework in which to understand their world (Deuteronomy 6:4-9). They will grow up seeing how God is intimately working in this life instead of being far off.

There is no better gift you can give your children than an understanding of the One who created them.

DEDICATION

To my children,
Emily and Josh,
and to those looking to

CONNECT THE DOTS

about the truth of God's word.

Let each be fully convinced in his own mind.
(Romans 14:5b)

CONTRIBUTIONS

There were many resources used to make this project a success, and we leaned heavily on four in particular. We recommend these resources to you for help in making sense of the Bible and *delighting in God's truth*.

> The ESV Study Bible. Crossway, Wheaton Illinois. 2008. www.esvbible.org
>
> Holman Bible Dictionary. Holman Bible Publishers, Nashville, Tennessee. 1991.
>
> Ryrie, Charles. The Ryrie Study Bible. Moody Press, Chicago. 1978.
>
> Strack, Jay. Impact Student Leadership Bible. Thomas Nelson, Nashville, Dallas, Mexico City, Rio De Janeiro. 2008. www.slulead.com

Thank you to our pastor, Dr. Willy Rice, who consistently provides opportunities for those on our church staff to express our gifts for the glory of God and for the good of His church.

Thank you to Dr. Aaron Walp, who believes in our God-given abilities and inspires us to do our best in all we set our mind to.

Thank you to our families, who support and sacrifice so that we can create and provide resources like this to Calvary Church, Clearwater and beyond.

50 Characters in the Bible

Aaron

Aaron, born to Amram and Jochebed, was the brother of Moses and was Israel's first high priest. Aaron had four sons with his wife Elisheba, but two of them died for their disobedience after they offered sacrifices with fire which God had not commanded them to make (Leviticus 10:1-2).

We don't know what Aaron did while Moses was in the wilderness for 40 years, but it is apparent that he kept the faith and kept in contact with Israel's leaders. When his brother returned, Aaron accompanied Moses, gathering the elders of Israel and serving as his spokesman before Pharaoh.

After the Israelites' exodus from Egypt, while Moses received the two tablets of testimony from God, Aaron yielded to the people's request to *make us gods who shall go before us*, making a golden calf from their possessions. About three thousand men died as a result, and Moses implored God to show mercy for their great sin (Exodus 32:1-20).

Later, during the 40 years of wandering in the desert, Aaron joined in Moses' sin at the waters of Meribah, where Moses disobeyed God's instruction. In doing so, Moses and Aaron demonstrated a desire to seize God's power for themselves. As a result, both Moses and Aaron would not lead the Israelites into the Promised Land (Numbers 20:7-13).

Abel

Abel, meaning "breath," was the second son of Adam and Eve. His name is associated with shortness of life because his life was cut short when his brother, Cain, murdered him out of envy (Genesis 4:8). God had received Abel's offering of the firstborn of his flock while rejecting Cain's offering of the fruit of the ground because Abel made his offering with the right attitude and in the proper manner (Hebrews 11:4). In Hebrews 12:24, Abel's blood is compared to Christ's blood. Abel's blood brought vengeance, while Christ's blood brings mercy.

Abel's life was brief, but his example should not be overlooked. He is to be remembered for his demonstration of faith and for being the first person to worship God correctly and was called righteous by Jesus Himself (Matthew 23:35). He was the first shepherd and the first martyr in human history.

Abraham

Abram, meaning "father is exalted" had his name changed by God to Abraham, meaning "father of a multitude." This name change signified a covenant between God and Abraham that the Bible continually refers to and is the family line that Gentiles (non-Jews) are grafted into upon becoming followers of Christ (Romans 11:11-31).

After Abraham's father, Terah, died, God called Abraham to migrate to Canaan and promised that he would father a great nation. Abraham, convinced by his wife Sarah, decided to speed up God's timing by taking her handmaid, Hagar, as a concubine (a secondary wife treated as property). Although Hagar conceived a son, Ishmael, he was not the one to become Abraham's heir.

Later, at the age of 90, Sarah conceived a son, Isaac (Genesis 17:17), who was the child of the promise that God had made with Abraham. He remarried in old age after the death of Sarah and had other children before dying at the age of 175.

God was known throughout the Bible as the God of Abraham and made His plan of redemption known to him. While the Hebrews took pride in being descendants of Abraham, the Apostle John made it clear that his blood line did not guarantee salvation to the Jews. Abraham is listed in the New Testament book of Hebrews for his faith in God's promise *that from one man, and him as good as dead, were born descendants as many as the stars of heaven and as many as the innumerable grains of sand by the seashore* (Hebrews 11:12, ESV).

Adam & Eve

Adam and Eve are our ancestral parents. Adam simply means "man" while Eve means "life-giving one." All of human history traces back to the creation of Adam and Eve. They were created by God; Adam from the dust of the ground and Eve from the rib of Adam. Man, created in God's image, was to have dominion over all the earth.

While Eve was deceived by the serpent's cunning (2 Corinthians 11:3), Adam was standing with her as she then turned and gave him the forbidden fruit to eat (Genesis 3:6). When they ate the fruit, *the eyes of both of them were opened, and they realized they were naked* (Genesis 3:7, NIV). This act of disobedience ushered sin into the world, and we have lived with its effects to this day.

This sin brought about judgment, not just on Adam and Eve, but on all creation (Genesis 3:14-19). God drove them from the Garden of Eden as an act of mercy, as He began making provision for the greatest rescue plan of all time which would eventually be realized in the person of Jesus (Romans 5:12-21). After leaving the garden, Adam and Eve had the world's first offspring (Genesis 4:1-2, 25, 5:4), which led to the growth of humanity.

Barnabas

Barnabas, meaning "son of prophecy," was a Levite and native of the island of Cyprus. His original name was Joseph before the disciples began calling him Barnabas. He sold the land he owned and gave the money to the apostles at the Jerusalem church (Acts 4:36).

Barnabas was the one who introduced Saul of Tarsus, later Paul, to the church, declaring the Damascus Road encounter with Jesus that Saul experienced (Acts 9:26-27). He chose Saul to accompany him to Syrian Antioch, where the Gospel could be freely preached to the Gentiles. They were both sent to Jerusalem to settle the question of how Gentiles could convert to Christ, and they testified to God's work among the Gentiles.

Later in their missionary journeys, Barnabas and Paul had a dispute over John Mark, Barnabas' nephew. They disagreed so sharply that they parted ways – Barnabas with John Mark to Cyprus and Paul with Silas to strengthen the churches throughout Syria and Cilicia (Acts 15:36-41).

Daniel

Daniel, meaning "God is judge," proved to keep the meaning of his name in full view when facing life's circumstances. He was taken captive by King Nebuchadnezzar and exiled from Judah to Babylon in 605 B.C. There, Daniel studied Babylonian culture and arts in his captor's attempt to remove all sense of his nationality or religion. They even changed his name to Belteshazzar. But Daniel determined in his heart to stay true to his God and not to defile himself by enjoying some of the king's delicacies and wine. God blessed him for his unwavering faithfulness and granted him favor with the chief of the eunuchs and gave him the ability to interpret dreams (Daniel 1-2).

Although God blessed Daniel, he faced opposition in his life. First, King Nebuchadnezzar made an image of gold that he ordered all officials to bow down and worship at its dedication festival. Daniel and his three friends refused and were subsequently thrown into the fiery furnace where God intervened. Not a hair on their head or a stitch of their clothing was singed. The king then made a decree that if anyone spoke against Daniel's God, they would be cut in pieces and their house made an ash heap (Ch. 3).

Daniel faced opposition again from other satraps, or governors, in the kingdom during King Darius' reign. The king was tricked into making a decree that anyone who petitioned anyone other than the king would be thrown into the lion's den. When Daniel learned of this, he went to his room and prayed as he was accustomed to doing. He was then thrown into the lion's den where *God sent His angel and shut the lions' mouths* (Daniel 6:22, ESV). God spared Daniel, but the same could not be said of the other satraps and their families. Once again, Daniel demonstrated unshakable faith in God.

David

When Saul, the first earthly king of Israel, failed to meet God's standards for a king, God sent Samuel to anoint a king from Jesse's family. The youngest son, David (meaning favorite or beloved), who tended sheep for his father, was the one that God had chosen (1 Samuel 16:1-13). David was the first king to unite Israel and Judah and the first to receive the promise of a royal messiah in his line (2 Samuel 7:11-16).

David's life was not without hardship, however. His life was threatened several times by Saul, even though he was loyal to the king. He lost his best friend, Jonathan, in war to the Philistines. David was the schemer of an unthinkable plan to have one of his soldiers, Uriah, murdered on the front line after impregnating the man's wife, Bathsheba (11-12:25). God took the child's life as a result of his sin. Later in his life, his son Absalom, revolted against David's throne, causing him more heartbreak.

Despite all of David's mistakes, God called David a man *after His own heart* (Acts 13:22). He left a legacy with the Jewish people that would never be forgotten. God spared the throne and the people for David's sake. And one day, long after David had died, a King from his family line was born in a manger in Bethlehem.

Elijah

Elijah, meaning "The Lord is my God," was a prophet from the Northern Kingdom of Tishbe in Gilead and was one of only two people in the Bible who did not die a physical death. He was a rugged, complex man who took Israel's role as God's chosen people very seriously. In a day when the worship of many gods was acceptable, he was unconditionally loyal to the one true God. Elijah lived during the reign of King Ahab.

His greatest miracle involved a faceoff between 450 prophets of Baal (fertility god) and 400 prophets of Asherah (fertility goddess). In a dramatic display, the false prophets called on their gods to no avail. After mocking the prophets and waiting from morning until late afternoon, Elijah called the people around, built an altar with twelve stones, and poured twelve large jars of water over the wood and the bull that made up the offering. He then called on the God of Abraham, Isaac, and Jacob. The fire of the Lord fell and consumed the entire altar, including the water that filled the trenches around the altar (1 Kings 18:20-40).

Elijah then ordered the false prophets to be slaughtered, which angered Jezebel, King Ahab's wife, who planned revenge. Elijah feared for his life and fled to Judah and begged God to take his life. God provided food for him to eat, and he *went in the strength of that food forty days and forty nights to Horeb* (1 Kings 19:8, ESV), where he heard God in a whisper commanding him to anoint Elisha as his successor. Elisha succeeded him as prophet just after Elijah was taken up into heaven in a chariot of fire (2 Kings 2:9-12).

Elisabeth

Elisabeth, meaning "my God has sworn an oath," a descendent of Aaron and wife of Zacharias, the priest, gave birth to John the Baptist, Jesus' cousin. Her worthiness to mother the one who prepared the way of the Lord is found in Luke 1:6: *righteous in God's eyes, careful to obey all of the Lord's commandments and regulations* (NLT).

Elisabeth was barren in her old age. When Mary, the mother of Jesus, was told that she would give birth to Christ, she was also told of Elisabeth's pregnancy, encouraging her that *nothing will be impossible with God* (Luke 1:37, ESV). Upon hearing this, Mary immediately went to visit Elisabeth and they encourage each other for about three months.

Elisha

Elijah's successor, Elisha, meaning "God is my salvation," asked for a double portion of Elijah's spirit before his predecessor was taken up into heaven. This reality was apparent to the sons of the prophets who acknowledged, "The spirit of Elijah rests on Elisha" (2 Kings 2:15, ESV), and it soon became apparent to everyone through the miracles he displayed: Elisha made bad water drinkable (2:19-22); saved a widow's children from becoming slaves (4:1-7); purified deadly stew (4:38-41); and made an ax-head float (6:5-7). In fact, a group of forty-two boys, who mocked the prophet of God, were attacked by two bears (2:23-24).

Perhaps Elisha's greatest miracle came to a Shunammite woman and her husband. The couple had graciously opened up their home to the prophet, making him a small room on the roof for him to use when he was in their town. Because of their kindness, they had been given a son by the Lord in response to Elisha's request. However, when working in the field one day, the boy died shortly after experiencing severe pain in his head. The mother found Elisha and begged for his help. After stretching himself out over the boy two times, the boy came back to life (4:8-37).

Elisha's powers did not end when he died. After Elisha was dead and buried, a dead man was thrown into his grave who, after touching his bones, revived and stood on his feet. Elisha performed many powerful and miraculous feats, yet he was sensitive enough to weep over the fate of Israel at the hands of Hazael (8:11-15).

Esther

Esther was an orphan raised by her uncle, Mordecai, in Persia during the time of King Ahasuerus. Because of her poverty, she had little material possessions, but she was a person of courage and kindness. The king had Queen Vashti dethroned for refusing to appear at a banquet the king had hosted. After competing against many beautiful women, Esther was chosen to become queen in her place because *she obtained grace and favor in his sight.* (Esther 2:17).

Mordecai instructed Esther to keep her Jewish identity a secret from the king and those in the palace (Esther 2:10). He discovered a plot by two eunuchs to kill the king, which he informed Esther of and thwarted the assassination attempt. Mordecai was despised by Haman, the prime minister, who devised a conspiracy against the Jews. The king issued a decree at the word of Haman that all Jews were to be annihilated (3:8-15).

Esther feared for her own life because to appear before the king without being summoned could result in her being put to death. Mordecai's famous response, *...who knows whether you have come to the kingdom for such a time as this?* (4:14) propelled Esther to approach the king, expose Haman's wicked plot, and save the Jewish people (ch. 5-8).

Ezra

Ezra, meaning "Yahweh helps," was a priest and scribe descended from Aaron. He lived during the reign of Artaxerxes, king of Persia and was known for his passionate love for God's word, and his commitment to hearing and obeying what it said. Ezra's purpose in going to Jerusalem was *to study and obey the Law of the Lord and to teach those decrees and regulations to the people of Israe"* (Ezra 7:10).

Ezra lived during the time that Nehemiah rebuilt the walls of Jerusalem. King Nebuchadnezzar had plundered Jerusalem, and the Jewish people were exiled (Jeremiah 52:28-30). However, King Cyrus of Persia then took over rule of Babylon and allowed his subjects to resume worship of their own gods. This was the perfect opportunity for the Jewish people to recapture what they had lost.

Ezra went to Jerusalem and read the law to the people as the wall was completed (Nehemiah 8:1-3, 8-12). God's word brought conviction and revival spread throughout Jerusalem. Ezra acted as a catalyst for change as the hearts of the people returned to worship the one, true God (Nehemiah 9).

Gideon

Gideon, meaning "one who cuts to pieces," was the son of Joash of the tribe of Manasseh. He was a judge in Israel for 40 years. Gideon was given the task of delivering the Israelites from the Midianites and Amalekites, desert nomads who were determined to raid the country. He was hiding on his farm when God called him, which was fitting for a coward from the weakest clan in his area and the most insignificant member of his family.

But God saw a man of faith whom He could use to deliver His people; for out of his weakness, he would be made strong (Hebrews 11:32-34). Gideon found a new identity when the all-powerful God turned him from a weakling to a warrior. He was a careful planner who did not move forward until he was sure of God's leading (Judges 6).

As He used Gideon to deliver the Israelites from the hands of the Midianites, God was concerned that the people might take credit for the victory, so He gave two tests to reduce the number of Gideon's army. Those who were afraid or who had knelt down to get a drink of water were sent home. The remaining 300 men were used to create an impression that the enemy was surrounded. The Midianites were thrown into confusion, the leaders were killed, and the threat of oppression was removed. Tragically, Gideon's greatest failure was that his faith in God was not passed on to his family (Judges 8:33-9:6).

Hezekiah

Hezekiah reigned as king of Judah, succeeding his father, King Ahaz, at the age of twenty-five. He reigned for twenty-nine years and did what was right in God's eyes. He began his reign by removing idols from The Temple and sanctifying temple vessels that were desecrated during his father's reign. He even removed and destroyed the bronze serpent that Moses had made (Numbers 21:4-9; 2 Kings 18:4). Because he followed the Lord, God was with him, bringing prosperity to him wherever he went.

In the fourth year of his reign, Hezekiah rebelled against the king of Assyria who had besieged Samaria. He knew that at some point he would have to face the Assyrians and began making preparations. He fortified the city of Jerusalem and even dug a tunnel through solid rock to access a water source from the spring of Gihon. He assembled an army and, after a decade, the king of Assyria, Sennacherib, attacked the fortified cities of Judah. Because Sennacherib boasted against the Lord, God sent an angel who killed 185,000 soldiers in the Assyrian camp. Sennacherib then went home where he was killed by his own sons (2 Kings 18-19).

At that time, the son of the king of Babylon, Merodach-Baladan, sent presents to Hezekiah when he heard that Hezekiah was deathly ill. God used the prophet Isaiah to heal him after hearing Hezekiah's prayer. Hezekiah then brought the king's son into his palace and showed him all his treasure, evidently being proud of his amassed prosperity (Proverbs 16:18). Isaiah warned Hezekiah that there would be a day when all of his accumulated wealth would be carried off to Babylon and that some of his sons would serve as eunuchs in the palace of the king of Babylon. Hezekiah received this as good news for he reasoned, *Will there not be peace and truth at least in my days?* (2 Kings 20:19).

Isaac

Isaac, meaning "laughter," was the only son of Abraham and Sarah. He was born of a promise from God (Genesis 17:17; 21:5), and as he grew, God directed Abraham to comply with Sarah's wish to ban Hagar and Ishmael, Isaac's half-brother saying, *Whatever Sarah says to you, do as she tells you, for through Isaac shall your offspring be named* (Genesis 21:12).

God used Isaac, Abraham's promised descendant, to test Abraham's faith. God commanded him to sacrifice Isaac in the land of Moriah. It can be deduced that Isaac willingly joined his dad as Abraham built the altar and bound his son on top of the wood. Abraham was old (100 years at the time of Isaac's birth), and Isaac could have easily escaped. However, he trusted his father who trusted in the Lord, and God stopped Abraham and provided a substitute sacrifice of a ram caught in a thicket by his horns (ch. 22).

Isaac grew up and married Rebekah, who had twin sons, Esau and Jacob. He was tricked into giving Jacob his blessing over his favored son, Esau. Isaac died near Hebron, about fifteen miles west of the Dead Sea, at the age of 180.

Isaiah

Isaiah, meaning "Yahweh saves," was born in Judah. He came from a noble family and was married with at least two sons. Isaiah received his call to be a prophet the same year that King Uzziah died. In his vision, Isaiah recorded, *I heard the voice of the Lord, saying: Whom shall I send, and who will go for Us? Then I said, 'Here am I! Send me* (Isaiah 6:8).

Isaiah was known as the golden prophet and prophesied during the reigns of Uzziah, Jotham, Ahaz, and Hezekiah. He was instrumental in influencing Hezekiah to remain neutral and not to join the rebellion against the Assyrians. He is remembered for his brilliant conception of God and for his prophecies of the Messiah. He prophesied that the Messiah: 1) would be born of a virgin (7:14); 2) would be the Prince of Peace (9:6) and; 3) would suffer for His people (Is. 53).

Issachar

Issachar, meaning "man for hire," was the ninth son of Jacob and the fifth son of Leah. He was the originator of the tribe of Issachar, which occupied the territory in the northern part of Palestine, just southwest of the Sea of Galilee. This tribe was not prominent in Israel's history. While almost nothing is known of his personal history, his descendants are listed in David's army at Hebron as *the sons of Issachar who had understanding of the times, to know what Israel ought to do…* (1 Chronicles 12:32).

Jacob

Jacob, son of Isaac and Rebekah, and grandson of Abraham, was the younger twin brother of Esau (Genesis 25:19-26). Although his name is built on the Hebrew noun for "heel" (meaning "he cheats"), God later changed his name to Israel. Jacob negotiated for his older brother's birthright by making him a pot of stew (25:27-34). When it came time for Isaac to bestow the blessing of the inheritance, Jacob disguised himself as his brother and stole the blessing (Genesis 27).

Jacob himself was cheated by his father-in-law, Laban, who tricked him into marrying his oldest daughter, Leah, before marrying his youngest daughter, Rachel. He ended up working 14 years for his wives, and the deception continued between the two men for another six years before Jacob left to return to his homeland. As Jacob returned to the Promised Land, he encountered a band of angels before heading south to meet Esau for the first time in 20 years. After crossing the Jabbok River, he wrestled with God until daybreak and would not let Him go. God refused to bless him until he said his name, "Jacob," which was likely a confession of his character. It was at this point that God changed his name to Israel (Genesis 29-32).

Jacob became the father of twelve sons, from which the nation of Israel's twelve tribes began. As his mother and father had done, Jacob favored one of his sons, Joseph, which led to jealousy, envy, and betrayal as the other eleven sons sold young Joseph into slavery and reported to their father that he was killed, torn into pieces by a wild beast (Genesis 37). A severe famine led the brothers to Egypt for food, where they found their brother ruling as second in command. Before he died, Jacob was reunited with Joseph in Goshen where he said, *Now let me die, since I have seen your face, because you are still alive* (Genesis 46:30, ESV).

James

James, son of Zebedee and brother of John (Mark 1:19), was one of the twelve disciples and, along with Peter and John, made up Jesus' inner circle. All three were present when Jesus raised Jairus' daughter from the dead (Luke 8:49-56), when Jesus was transfigured on the mountain (Matthew 17:1-8), and when Jesus agonized in the Garden of Gethsemane just before being betrayed by Judas (Matthew 26:36-46).

This James was not the brother of Jesus and likely did not author the book of James. Jesus called the two brothers "Sons of Thunder" (Mark 3:17), which fit them well as their response to Jesus being rejected in a Samaritan village was *Lord, do you want us to command fire to come down from heaven and consume them, just as Elijah did?* (Luke 9:54). However, the two's motives were less than pure however, so Jesus used the opportunity to teach the lesson that being great means being a servant of all (Mark 10:35-45).

James was the first of the twelve disciples to be martyred. King Herod pierced him with a sword, killing him during his persecution of the church (Acts 12:1-2).

Jeremiah

Jeremiah, son of Hilkiah, was called to be prophet in the thirteenth year of King Josiah's reign, although God ordained him to be prophet long before that time (Jeremiah 1:2, 5). More is known about Jeremiah's personal life than any other prophet. He is known as the weeping prophet (9:1) penning his book near the end of his ministry. He would never marry or have a family of his own at God's instruction (16:2).

Jeremiah's calling as prophet was not an easy one. He lived in constant friction with the leaders of his day, as he pronounced God's judgment for the sin of the people. He was convicted of treason (38:1-6), accused of lying (43:1-3), and was threatened to be put to death because he had prophesied against Judah (26:7-15). Although Jeremiah wanted to quit (20:7-18), he determined to stay faithful to God's call on his life. He was an example of one who did not allow his circumstances to determine his obedience to God. He prophesied for over forty years. While it is not known when Jeremiah died, Jewish tradition says that he was stoned to death in Egypt (Hebrews 11:37).

Jesus

Jesus, meaning "anointed one" is the central character in the Bible and is introduced in the first chapter of Genesis as Creator (Genesis 1:26-27; Colossians 1:15-17). He is not only the chief figure in the Bible, but is also the most significant Person of all time. Jesus is the second Person of the Trinity – God the Father, Son, and Holy Spirit. While He is equal with the Father, He is also submissive to the Father as He was sent to die for the sins of the world (1 John 4:14).

Jesus was conceived supernaturally to Mary by the Holy Spirit about 2,000 years ago. He lived a perfect life, although tempted by Satan and was crucified, buried, and rose again. In this, He became the perfect sacrifice for sin, conquering sin and death once and for all (1 John 2:2). Throughout His earthly ministry, He taught people how they should live and contested the religious leaders of the day, particularly the Pharisees.

Jesus is now with the Father in heaven actively petitioning on our behalf (Romans 8:34) and preparing a place for those who have put their faith in Him (John 14:2-3). He will come again to gather His own and to judge the world. Those who have not put their faith in Jesus will have to pay the penalty for their sin in hell (Romans 6:23; Matthew 13:36-43). Those who have put their faith in Jesus trust that He has paid their penalty by dying on the cross (Romans 10:9-11). They will be judged and rewarded for their works here on earth (2 Corinthians 5:10).

Job

Job, meaning "the persecuted one," was a wealthy nomad in Uz, a land southeast of Palestine (Job 1:1). It is likely that he lived during the time of the patriarchs, since Job offered his own sacrifices (instead of a priest), and the book of Job does not mention the Law or the Exodus from Egypt.

A common belief today is that suffering is a result of God's judgment on a person for their sin. This belief was apparently true in Job's day as well. While Job lived a life of integrity, Satan challenged his righteousness, with God's permission, attacking his wealth and his family. Job lost everything but his wife and his health in one day. When Job did not blame God, Satan requested permission to attack his personal health, which God granted. He was infected with painful boils from head to toe, but in all of this, Job refused to blame God (Ch. 1-2).

Job wondered why he was ever born (3:1-26), and his friends tried to convince him that God was punishing him for his sin (Ch. 4-11). Job's three friends, Aliphaz, Bildad, and Zophar grew increasingly frustrated as he held fast to his integrity. God finally spoke, asking Job a series of questions about his ability to do better as Creator and Sustainer of the world. To both, Job responded, "No," which pleased the Lord (Ch. 38-41). God rebuked Job's three friends and instructed Job to pray for them. In the end, God restored all Job's fortunes and gave him even more children (42:10-17).

Job was recognized by Ezekiel as one of Israel's most righteous ancestors, along with Noah and Daniel, and James refers to Job as an example of God's display of compassion for those who endure.

John

John, meaning "God has been gracious," was the son of Zebedee and the brother of James. He and his brother were among the first called disciples of Jesus as they prepared to fish with their father in the Sea of Galilee (Matthew 4:21-22).

John, along with Peter and James, made up Jesus' inner circle. They were all three present when Jesus raised Jairus' daughter from the dead (Luke 8:49-56), when Jesus was transfigured on the mountain (Matthew 17:1-8), and when Jesus agonized in the Garden of Gethsemane just before being betrayed by Judas (Matthew 26:36-46). Peter and John would be the two that would prepare the Passover meal for Jesus and the disciples the night he was betrayed (Luke 22:8).

John has been attributed to writing five books in the New Testament – the Gospel of John, the three epistles, and Revelation. John, known as the Beloved Disciple, purposed to convince people to believe in Jesus and inherit eternal life.

John the Baptist

John the Baptist, a New Testament prophet born to Zechariah and Elisabeth (Luke 1:5-80), preached a message of repentance and baptism. He was known as the one who prepared the way of the Lord (Luke 3:3-17). He was Jesus' cousin, and he baptized Jesus "to fulfill all righteousness" (Matthew 3:13-17).

Before John the Baptist's ministry began, he lived in the wilderness and ate wild locusts and honey. He dressed as a prophet, wearing camel's hair and a leather belt (Matthew 3:4; 2 Kings 1:8). John's message was clear – judgment was coming and the people needed to repent of their sins to prepare for the coming Messiah.

John the Baptist, like Jesus, had disciples (Mark 2:18). They attended to him while he was in prison (Matthew 11:2-3). Although King Herod was afraid of John, he had him beheaded at the request of Herodias through her daughter, who danced before the king on his birthday (Mark 6:14-29). Jesus said of him, *among those born of women there has not risen one greater than John the Baptist* (Matthew 11: 11).

Jonah

Jonah, meaning "dove," is one of the best known Minor Prophets in the Bible. He prophesied during the reign of Jeroboam, predicting the restoration of the Northern Kingdom and expressing God's desire to save His people although they were wicked (2 Kings 14:25-27).

Jonah disobeyed God's word to warn the people of Nineveh of His coming judgment, because he knew that God was merciful. He attempted to flee to Tarshish by boat (Jonah 1:1-3), but a violent storm threatened all aboard the sailing vessel, and he instructed the mariners to throw him into the sea (1:4-16). God prepared a fish to swallow Jonah, not as punishment for his disobedience but to save him (1:17-2:1). Jonah was in the belly of the fish for three days and three nights (which would foreshadow Jesus' death and resurrection (Luke 11:29-32).

Jonah reluctantly warned Nineveh of their need to repent with one sentence as he walked into the city: *"Forty days from now Nineveh will be destroyed!" All of the people of Nineveh responded with a repentant heart* (Jonah 3:4-6, NLT). God relented from His anger, which only served to fuel Jonah's anger. As a result, Jonah missed out on the blessing of rejoicing over those who repented.

Joseph

Joseph, meaning "adding," was the eleventh of twelve sons of Jacob (Israel) and was the first son of Jacob's beloved wife Rachel, which may be the reason that he was favored above all his brothers. He was given the famous *coat of many colors*. While Joseph was adored by his parents, he was hated by his brothers because of the preferential treatment he received (Genesis 37:3).

After sharing his dreams of dominance with his brothers, Joseph was sold into slavery as part of a plot to get rid of him (37:12-36). Joseph was then taken to Egypt where he was purchased by Potiphar, where he became a trusted slave. Because he would not have sexual relations with Potiphar's wife, he was wrongly accused and thrown into prison, where he found favor with the keeper of the prison. God granted him the ability to interpret dreams, the most important dream being Pharaoh's dream of seven years of abundance and seven years of famine. Eventually, Joseph would find himself second in command over all of Egypt (ch. 39-41).

The seven years of famine caused people from surrounding countries to go to Egypt to buy food, including Joseph's brothers. While the brothers did not recognize Joseph, he recognized them. His dreams were fulfilled – his brothers bowed down to him. Through a series of events, Joseph disclosed his identity and stressed to his guilt-ridden brothers *God sent me before you to preserve for you a remnant on earth* (Genesis 45:7).

Joseph, Foster Father of Jesus

Joseph, a descendent of David, was the husband of Mary, the mother of Jesus (Luke 2:4-5). He was a carpenter who was regarded as the foster father of Jesus. Few words are written about Joseph in the Bible, but he is portrayed as a man of character and deep conviction. God set him apart for a specific purpose that would require immediate obedience and decisive action. Joseph proved to be the right man for the job.

When Joseph learned of Mary's pregnancy, he planned to quietly divorce her, knowing she would be accused of adultery, punishable by stoning her to death (Deuteronomy 22:20-21). An angel of the Lord appeared to Joseph in a dream urging him to take Mary as his *wife ...for the child within her was conceived by the Holy Spirit.* The angel also instructed him that the child's name would be Jesus, because He would save God's people from their sins (Matthew 1:20-21, NLT; Isaiah 7:14).

Because of a census that went out, Joseph took Mary to his ancestral home, Bethlehem in Judea, to be registered. It was there, in a manger, that the Christ Child was born. Joseph was present for Jesus' circumcision and dedication in the Temple (Luke 2:8-33). It is likely that Joseph died prior to Jesus' public ministry because he is not mentioned later in the Gospel accounts.

Joshua

Joshua, meaning "Yahweh is salvation" is translated "Jesus" in Greek. He succeeded Moses as leader of the Israelites and led them into the Promised Land following Moses' death. It took a man of his great character to succeed such a man as Moses.

Joshua was born in Egypt while the Israelites were enslaved to Egyptian rule, to the tribe of Ephraim under the name Hoshea. Moses was responsible for changing his name to Joshua when he was sent out with the others to spy out the land of Canaan (Numbers 13:8). Caleb was the only other spy to return with Joshua giving a positive report about what they saw. Because of the Israelites' opposition to taking the Promised Land, these two were the only adults who were allowed to enter the land God gave them 40 years later (Numbers 14:28-30,38).

Joshua would serve as Moses' general in battle and accompanied Moses on the mountain when he received the Law from God (Exodus 17:8-13; 32:17). God chose him to succeed Moses long before Moses' death (Numbers 27:15-23). Throughout his life, Joshua acted as a military, political, and spiritual leader, using his quiet demeanor to challenge God's people by word and example. God renewed his covenant with Israel through Joshua, and his legacy is recorded in Joshua 24:31 *Israel served the Lord all the days of Joshua...*(ESV).

Josiah

Josiah, meaning "God heals," succeeded his father Amon as King of Judah (2 Chronicles 33:21-25). Unlike his father, he did what was right in the eyes of the Lord and in the eighth year of his reign, began to seek God. Four years later, he began to purge the kingdom of altars to foreign gods, specifically Baal, the fertility God of Canaan (2 Chronicles 34:1-7).

Six years later, Hilkiah, the high priest, found The Book of the Law and gave it to the king's scribe, Shaphan. The scribe brought it to the king and began to read it aloud. Upon hearing its message, Josiah tore his clothes and humbled himself. He then appointed certain people to inquire of the Lord on his behalf, because he knew that they had not heeded God's word. God assured Josiah that because he humbled himself, he would not see the calamity that God would bring on the inhabitants of the land (2 Chronicles 34:8-28).

Josiah was remembered for making the most dramatic religious reforms in Israel's history. While the Bible is silent about the remaining years of his life, the Bible records *Neither before nor after Josiah was there a king like him who turned to the Lord as he did...* (2 Kings 23:25, NIV). He died in battle after being shot by an archer. All Judah and Jerusalem mourned for Josiah including Jeremiah, the prophet (2 Chronicles 35:20-25).

Judah

Judah, meaning "praise YAHWEH," was the fourth son of Jacob and the originator of the tribe of Judah. While Judah is rarely mentioned as a central figure of the book of Genesis, chapter 38 reveals the seductive plot of his daughter-in-law, Tamar, who gave birth to his twin boys, Perez and Zerah.

In pronouncing a blessing over Judah before his death, Jacob proclaimed, *Judah, you are he whom your brothers shall praise; Your hand shall be on the neck of your enemies; Your father's children shall bow down before you* (Genesis 49:8). Through Judah runs the genealogical line that leads to Jesus (Matthew 1:2-3).

Lazarus

Lazarus, meaning "one who God helps," was the brother of Mary and Martha. The three siblings were all personal friends of Jesus, which may explain why Jesus frequented the small village of Bethany, just outside Jerusalem, where they lived. The disciples knew of Jesus' affection and love for Lazarus and his two sisters referring to His love for them often.

One of Jesus' most amazing miracles concerned his friend, Lazarus. The disciples informed Jesus that Lazarus was seriously ill, but Jesus waited two days before leaving to visit him. During this time, Lazarus died, and when Jesus arrived, he had been in the tomb for four days. Jesus had prophesied days earlier that Lazarus' sickness would lead to the glory of God. While the two sisters were mourning the loss of their brother and other Jews were gathered to comfort them, Jesus was brought to the tomb, and He ordered that the stone be rolled away. Jesus then commanded in a loud voice, *Lazarus, come forth*. Lazarus then came out with his grave clothes still on him and, as a result, many people believed in Jesus (John 11:1-45, NASB).

Luke

Luke, the only Gentile writer of the New Testament, authored the third Gospel and the Book of Acts and was a close friend of Paul (Colossians 4:11-14). Luke's name appears in the New Testament only three times; all three mention Luke's presence with, and are in epistles written by, Paul from prison (Colossians 4:14; 2 Timothy 4:11; Philemon 24). In fact, many people believe that Luke wrote his two books of the Bible while in prison with Paul in Rome.

Early church records indicate that Luke was from Antioch, although Luke adopted Philippi as his home. He was a physician who carefully studied the eyewitness accounts of the life of Jesus, which aided him in writing the only chronological Gospel account.

Mary Magdalene

Mary Magdalene was from an important agricultural, fishing, and trade center of Galilee called Magdala. She was one of several women who followed Jesus. She was healed of several demons, which indicated that she might have some serious physical or spiritual sickness. Mary Magdalene followed Jesus to the cross, she observed the crucifixion (Mark 15:40) and burial of Christ (15:47), and she witnessed the empty tomb (16:1-8) and the resurrected Jesus (16:9).

Mary, Mother of Jesus

Mary, mother of Jesus and wife of Joseph, was a young girl (maybe 12-14 years old) when she became pregnant with her first Son. She was a virgin when she gave birth to the Christ Child (Matthew 1:24-25), but she was not a perpetual virgin, as she had other children (Matthew 12:46-47, 13:55). Mary was a person of character and innocence, highly favored by God (Luke 1:28), but the Bible's focus is on the Son, not the mother.

Although Mary was God's servant (Luke 1:38), life was full of hardships as she experienced the reality of being an unwed mother (Matthew 1:18), she almost lost her fiancé (Matthew 1:19), she could have been stoned to death (Deuteronomy 22:20), and she witnessed her oldest Son's brutal betrayal and execution (Mark 14:27-15:47). Mary experienced every joy and every sorrow as the mother of the Savior. As Simeon prophesied in the Temple, a sword pierced Mary's own soul (Luke 2:35).

The Bible last recorded Mary at the foot of the cross in John 19, fitting for God's servant. Just before Jesus died on the cross (vv.26-27), He showed concern for his mother and His disciple and brother, John, by encouraging them to care for each other. Mary was the only person who was with Jesus for His entire earthly life – from birth to death.

Mordecai

Mordecai, descendent of King Saul's family, was the adoptive father of Esther (Esther 2:7), Queen of Persia (2:18).

He was largely responsible for her rise to power and for the salvation of the Jews in Persia. He discovered a plot to kill Ahasuerus, the King of Persia, which he made known to Esther, saving the king's life (2:19-23). He would not be rewarded for this deed until a later time.

Mordecai refused to pay homage to one of the king's officials, the evil Haman, a descendent of the Amalekite King Agag (3:2-6). As a result, Haman devised a plot to destroy the Jewish race, sealed with the king's signet ring 3:7-15). Haman had gallows prepared to hang Mordecai, for he especially hated him (5:9-14). Mordecai entreated Esther to action. He proposed that God might have made her queen to save His people (4:13-14), and that she should not suppose that she was safe, for she was a Jew.

During this time, Mordecai was honored for his earlier exposure of the assassination plot against the king. Esther exposed Haman for the adversary he was at a banquet she had prepared. Haman was hanged on the gallows he had made ready for Mordecai (7:1-10), who was appointed second in command in the kingdom (10:2).

Moses

After the time of Joseph, the Israelites grew in number and their population in Egypt became very large. A new king came to power – one who had never heard of Joseph and one who was very harsh to God's people (Exodus 1). At this time, Moses was born and was kept hidden because newborn male infants were being put to death by order of the king. After three months, Moses' family sent him down the river, and he was rescued by Pharaoh's daughter, who raised him as her own (2:1-10).

Moses grew up as an Egyptian and was educated in the best schools Egypt had to offer. He was quite an impressive young man. At the age of 40, he witnessed an

Egyptian abusing an Israelite, and he stepped in, killing the Egyptian. Moses thought that the Israelites would see that God might deliver them through him, but they did not. Instead, they accused him of wanting to kill them as he had killed the Egyptian. Moses then fled to Midian, where he seemed happy as a desert shepherd for 40 years (2:11-25).

But at the age of 80, God spoke to Moses out of a burning bush and ordered him back to Egypt to deliver God's people (Exodus 3). After ten plagues on Egypt and the institution of The Passover, Pharaoh agreed to release the Israelites from slavery. Moses led them across the Red Sea on dry ground where Pharaoh and his army perished as the waters came crashing down on them (Exodus 7-14). They wandered in the wilderness for 40 years due to their disbelief that God would give them the Promised Land. Although Moses did not lead the Israelites into the Promised Land for not believing God (Numbers 21:3), the Bible records *There has not arisen in Israel a prophet like Moses, whom the Lord knew face to face* (Deuteronomy 34:10).

Nehemiah

Nehemiah, meaning "God encourages," was an organized and dynamic leader who had a reputation for getting things done, which is why God used him to rebuild the walls of Jerusalem. Nehemiah was cupbearer to the king, an office of trust, usually not given to a captive, which testified to his character and standing.

When Nehemiah learned what had become of Jerusalem (the city lay in ruins), he wept for days and repented before God (Nehemiah 1:4-11). As he returned to Jerusalem and began to repair the walls of the city with the permission of the king, he carefully crafted a successful plan. He experienced trouble from outsiders, Sanballat and his friends, who tried to stop the work (Ch. 4).

Nehemiah also experienced trouble from within as economic strain led to a work shortage and high rates of interest that the people charged each other. Nehemiah quickly responded, fixing the problem and even providing financial assistance to those in need (Ch. 5). Nehemiah completed reconstruction of the wall in fifty-two days (6:15).

Nehemiah was a legendary leader whose theology was highly practical. His relationship with God affected every area of his life and was evident to all. He went on to make several reforms in Jerusalem which was an answer to his prayer *Let your servant prosper this day...* (Nehemiah 1:11).

Noah

Noah, son of Lamech and descendent of Adam of the line of Seth, was a just man who walked with God. During the time of Noah humans were continually evil (Genesis 6:5) to the point that God said, *...I am sorry I ever made them* (Genesis 6:7, NLT). But Noah found grace in God's eyes, and God gave him specific instructions for building the ark that would deliver his family from the impending flood (Genesis 6:8-21).

Noah followed God's instructions completely (6:22), and the time of the Great Flood came. The Lord directed Noah with his family into the ark along with two of every unclean animal and seven of every clean animal. After seven days, the rain started and lasted for 40 days (7:1-12). Noah sent out a raven and a dove to judge when the waters receded. After Noah and his family exited the ark, he sacrificed clean animals as a burnt offering on an altar he built. God then promised never to destroy the earth again in that manner and placed a rainbow in the sky as a seal of that covenant (8:15-9:17).

While God made a covenant with Noah, the evil intentions of man still lingered with those who were saved by the ark. Noah was no exception. Once on dry ground again, he farmed and got drunk with wine from a vineyard he planted. After he passed out, exposing himself in his tent, Ham, his son, saw him and left him to go tell his brothers, Shem and Japheth. Out of respect, they covered their father. Noah blessed the two for their discretion while he cursed his younger son. Noah lived 350 more years and died at the age of 950.

Paul

Through his contributions to the New Testament (author of 13 books), the Apostle Paul plays a significant role in helping us understand the character of the early church. Paul's Hebrew name was Saul, but because he was born in the Roman city of Tarsus, he was afforded the opportunity to claim Roman citizenship, thus giving him a Roman name as well. Growing up in a Jewish family, he was well trained in the scriptures and Jewish tradition, learning to read and write by copying selections of Scripture. Just as every Jewish boy, Paul learned a trade (tent-making) and would use it as a means of provision (Acts 18:3). As he grew older, he went to Jerusalem to study under the famous rabbi, Gamaliel, to continue his passionate study and pursuit of knowing God (Acts 22:3).

Paul was well acquainted with the Gospel and the Christian movement that he witnessed among his people, and he actively worked against it. He was present and approved of Stephen's execution (Acts 7:58; 8:1). He *persecuted this Way to the death, binding and delivering to prison both men and women* (Acts 22:4, ESV). On his way to arrest more Jews who had put faith in Jesus, he encountered Jesus on the road to Damascus and was soon after converted to Christianity. Paul's radical conversion is one of the strongest proofs of the resurrected Christ.

After Paul's conversion, he led three missionary journeys that took him almost ten years to complete. During that time, he planted approximately fourteen churches and spread the Gospel throughout modern-day Turkey, Syria, and Israel. When Paul returned to Jerusalem for the last time, he was arrested and imprisoned for his faith in the resurrection of Jesus and his calling to reach the Gentiles (Acts 22:21-22). He was eventually transferred to Rome where many believe he was executed.

Peter

Peter, meaning "rock," formerly known as Simon, was a leader of the disciples and frequently acted as the spokesperson for the group. The Bible records much of Peter's familial background, giving us key information about his life. He was from Bethsaida (John 1:44) and was a Galilean fishermen (Mark 1:16). Peter was married and lived with his family in Capernaum (Mark 1:21, 29-31) at the time Jesus called his disciples to follow Him. Andrew, his brother, was instrumental in bringing him to Christ (John 1:35-42).

As a disciple, Peter typically asked Jesus the questions that the rest of the disciples wanted to ask but did not. Several times throughout His ministry, Jesus singled Peter out while instructing His disciples. Peter was one of the first in recorded history to proclaim who Jesus was: *You are the Messiah, the Son of the living God* (Matthew 16:16, NIV). As a part of Jesus' inner circle of three – Peter, James, and John – Peter witnessed the Transfiguration, which was the transformation of Jesus in His appearance with Moses and Elijah (Matthew 17:1-8).

Jesus challenged Peter's audacious claim that he would never fall away with an admonition that foretold of his denial of Christ before the rooster would crow three times that same night (Matthew 26:33-35, 69-75). When this came true, Peter was distraught over his cowardice as he witnessed the crucifixion of his Savior. However, when Jesus rose from the dead, He appeared to Peter and reaffirmed His love for Peter and re-commissioned him to service (John 21). Peter's ministry to the early church was significant as he was instrumental in helping hold them together as Christianity began to spread.

Rebekah

Rebekah, meaning "looped cord for tying young animals," was Isaac's wife (Genesis 24:67) and was the mother of Jacob and Esau (25:25-26). Like many names in the Old Testament, Rebekah's name provides insight into her occupation as a shepherdess.

Rebekah had a reputation for being decisive and for taking initiative. She was a willing servant and provided water for Abraham's servant and his camels (24:13-21). She was hospitable to the servant, a total stranger, offering him a place to lodge for the night (24:25). She even responded quickly in obedience to God's call to be Isaac's wife (24:34-61).

Rebekah was not perfect, however, and schemed with her favorite son, Jacob, to steal Isaac's blessing from the older twin, Esau. Isaac was not able to distinguish between the two sons due to his old age and fading eyesight. Rebekah prepared a delicious meal for Jacob to present to his father while Jacob disguised himself as his brother (27:1-29). In order to protect Jacob from Esau's vengeance, she sent her favorite son out of the country to her brother's household (27:41-46).

Ruth

Ruth, the daughter-in-law of Naomi, was a woman of virtue and, above all, commitment. She refused to leave her mother-in-law's side even though Naomi urged her to remain in her homeland. One of the most beautiful demonstrations of loyalty is in Ruth's reply to Naomi: *Don't ask me to leave you and turn back. Wherever you go, I will go; wherever you live, I will live. Your people will be my people, and your God will be my God* (Ruth 1:16).

With this decision, Ruth embraced the God of Israel as her own and learned about the God Naomi believed in and served. Naomi taught Ruth about the One True God, and she showed by her example that taking care of another's needs can help us through our own pain. Ruth more than likely learned to be a virtuous woman from Naomi (3:10).

In order to make a living, Ruth went into the fields to pick up wheat that was left behind for the impoverished. She providentially ended up in Boaz's field. He was kind to her and ensured her safety, as he was actually the kinsman redeemer for her family (2:1-23). Naomi and Ruth took a risky step to make their intentions known to Boaz, who responded with favor and was willing to marry her (Ch. 3-4). Ruth is named in the genealogy of Jesus in Matthew 1:5.

Samson

While Samson is known for his incredible strength, there is much to learn from his weakness. Samson, meaning "of the sun," was the son of Manoah of the tribe of Dan, and had been dedicated to the Lord by his parents (Judges 13:3-7). However, Samson did not take this calling to heart and chose instead to live a careless life, participating in many ungodly acts. He disregarded the prohibition of approaching a dead body and ate honey from inside the carcass (14:8-9). He committed an immoral act with a harlot (16:1) and with Delilah (16:4-20).

Samson, a strong man with no self-control, had a weakness for women. In fact, his mishaps were often brought on by his relationships with Philistine women, none more destructive than his love affair with Delilah. Samson was deceived by Delilah and he did not resist her persistence in revealing to her the secret behind his power. He relented and disclosed his secret to Delilah (16:17). Samson was then captured, and she was rewarded with eleven hundred pieces of silver by each of the lords of the Philistines.

Samson's power did not come from his long hair, as he claimed, but from the Spirit of the Lord (14:6, 19, 15:14, 16:28-29). After years of humiliation (16:21), he eventually got the opportunity to take vengeance against the Philistines. The Bible records that Samson killed more Philistines in his death than he did during his life. Although he never freed the Israelites from captivity, he is mentioned in Hebrews for demonstrating faith in his dying act (Hebrews 11:32).

Samuel

Samuel, meaning "God is exalted," filled many roles in Israel's history. He was an answer to prayer by his barren mother, Hannah, and was dedicated to the Lord before his birth. Samuel lived during a time of great transition for the nation of Israel and served as judge (1 Samuel 7:3-4), first prophet (3:20), first king-maker (Ch. 8-10), priest (2:26-36), counselor to the king (13:13-15), and father (8:1-3). His life can be summed up in one word: obedience.

Samuel's ministry began when he was just a child (2:18-19, 3:1-21). His first word from the Lord was a message to his mentor, Eli, that God had rejected him and his descendants because of the sins of his sons. The Bible records *The Lord was with him and let none of his words fall to the ground* (1 Samuel 3:19, ESV).

The sin of Samuel's sons led the people of Israel to cry out for a king (8:3-5). God chose Samuel to anoint Saul as first earthly king of Israel, although Samuel warned the people what this would mean (8:10-18). Ultimately, God rejected Saul for his disobedience (Ch. 15), and Samuel anointed David as King of Israel (Ch. 16) before his death (Ch. 25).

Saul, Son of Kish

Saul, meaning "asked for," was the son of Kish from the tribe of Benjamin (Jacob's youngest son) and the first earthly king of Israel. Saul was chosen by God and anointed secretly by Samuel to govern the Israelites (1 Samuel 9:15-17). Despite some skepticism by the people, Saul demonstrated great leadership, saving the city of Jabesh-gilead from opposition and securing his place in the people's hearts as their king. He was formally crowned king at Gilgal.

It soon became apparent that Saul was moved more by his circumstances rather than trusting and obeying God's command. He used religious ceremony in an attempt to gain God's favor, which had the opposite effect (13:8-15). God did not tolerate his disobedience and, after a second incident, God rejected Saul completely. Samuel reminded him that God had anointed him as king to lead the people to obey God; not to be led astray by them (15:17).

The Spirit of the Lord then left Saul and was replaced by a harmful spirit which tormented him continuously. One of Saul's servants suggested that David soothe the king by playing the lyre whenever the harmful spirit came upon him. This pleased Saul, and David found favor in his eyes.

However, this soured shortly thereafter when Saul became jealous of David after he defeated Goliath. Saul attempted to kill David several times in fits of rage and even slaughtered the priests at Nob trying to get to David (22:17-19). Finally, his reign ended as he "took his own sword and fell upon it *to avoid being mistreated and killed by the Philistines* (Ch. 31).

Solomon

Solomon, meaning "peaceful," was David's tenth son and the second son of David and Bathsheba (after the death of their first-born). Solomon was crowned king by his father after Bathsheba and Nathan, the prophet, thwarted a plan by Adonijah, the fourth son of David to take the throne (1 Kings 2:10-25).

Solomon reigned forty years and is remembered most for his wisdom (granted by God at his request), recording three thousand proverbs and over a thousand songs. His most well-known display of wisdom came by the account of two prostitutes who claimed rights to a baby (1 Kings 3:16-28).

Because Solomon did not ask for riches, but for wisdom, God also granted him great wealth. In fact, Israel experienced its greatest prosperity and expansion during his reign. He was known for the wealth he generated through trade and administrative organization. His wisdom allowed him to see the importance of fortifying many important cities under his control. As a result of his decisiveness and action, these cities were better protected. He also built store-cities for amassing supplies and established military bases for his chariots and horsemen. Whatever Solomon desired to build, God granted him success, including his house and the Temple of the Lord (1 Kings 9:10-19).

Solomon's wisdom was evident in every area of his life except one – he had 700 wives and 300 concubines. These women led his heart astray, eventually leading him away from total devotion to God, unlike his father, David (1 Kings 11:33). In fact, Solomon not only allowed his wives to worship their gods, but he also built altars designed to offer sacrifices to them (1 Kings 11:6-8). As a result, God stripped the kingdom from his son, dividing the nation of Israel (1 Kings 11:26-40).

Stephen

Stephen, meaning "crown," was the first Christian martyr, stoned to death following his sermon to the Jewish Sanhedrin (Acts 7:54-60). Stephen was described as a man full of faith and power (6:8). So compelling were his declarations that Jesus was the Messiah that no one could dispute him (6:10).

The Jewish leaders (Pharisees) present that day did not need to win the argument; they only wanted to keep Stephen quiet. They succeeded by inducing men to bring false charges against him. He was arrested and brought in front of the high priest, where he addressed the court. Stephen spoke of Abraham, Joseph, and Moses before speaking about the history of rebellion in the Jewish history. He followed this with a harsh accusation, *You stubborn people! You are heathen at heart and deaf to the truth. Must you forever resist the Holy Spirit? That's what your ancestors did, and so do you!* (7:51, NLT).

Stephen was stoned immediately after his indictment of the Jewish leaders, and one of those consenting to his murder was Saul, later Paul. Stephen was among the first of those who took seriously the call of the Great Commission to take the Gospel to the entire world.

Timothy

Timothy, meaning "honoring God," was the friend and trusted servant leader of Paul. He was raised by his mother Eunice and his Greek father. While his father's faith in Christ is not mentioned, his mother and grandmother, Lois, taught him the scriptures (2 Timothy 1:5, 3:14-15). Although Timothy may have been shy, according to Paul, he was a true son in the faith (2 Timothy 1:2, 7).

Timothy was a native of Lystra and may have been converted on Paul's first missionary journey (Acts 14:6-23). Timothy was well spoken of by the believers (Acts 16:1-2). Paul gave Timothy many responsibilities as he traveled and even sent Timothy in his place when unable to travel or imprisoned (1 Corinthians 4:17, Philippians 2:20-22). So great was Paul's affection for Timothy that he called him to be with him just before he died (2 Timothy 4:9).

Uzziah

Uzziah (also known as Azariah) meaning "God is might," became King of Judah when he was sixteen years old. He reigned for fifty-two years and did what was right in God's eyes. He made war with the Philistines and tore down their walls. His fame began to spread as he built towers and military outposts. He refortified the walls of Jerusalem with towers (2 Chronicles 26:1-15).

Uzziah is known for being the "leper king" (2 Kings 14:1-7). God struck Uzziah with leprosy for his arrogance and display of anger toward the priests when they admonished him for his presumption concerning a religious ordinance. He had leprosy to the day of his death. As a leper, he was denied burial in the royal tombs at Jerusalem. (2 Chronicles 26:16-23).

12 Facts About the Dirty Dozen

This list is designed to be a quick reference guide for you to use when considering the vilest characters in the Bible. We can all learn lessons from these characters about traits that we should avoid so we do not fall into the trap of thinking more highly of ourselves than we should (Romans 12:3). Heed the stories of those below taking care in how you choose to live (Haggai 1:7).

Absalom

Ahab

Baal

Cain

Haman

Herod the Great

Jezebel

Judas

Pharaoh

Pharisees

Pilate

Satan

Absalom (2 Samuel 13-19:8)

- Personal name meaning "father of peace"

- Third son of King David

- The most handsome and cunning of all David's sons (2 Samuel 14:25)

- Ambition led him to want King David's throne at any cost

- Sister Tamar was raped by their brother Amnon, which led him down a bitter path of hate and vengeance (2 Samuel 13)

- Seized an opportunity to become first in line to the throne and exacted revenge upon Amnon by having him murdered

- Fled from David, spending three years in Geshur

- Returned to the kingdom after David forgave him for his vengeful actions against Amnon

- Stole the hearts of the people by sowing subtle seeds of doubt against King David (2 Samuel 15:6)

- Led a rebellion to assassinate his father, driving David from the kingdom

- Despised his father so liberally that he assumed the throne by going into "his father's concubines in the sight of all Israel" (2 Samuel 16:22)

- After 20,000 of his men were killed in a battle against his father, Absalom got caught up in a terebinth tree by his hair and was killed (2 Samuel 18:1-19)

Ahab (1 Kings 16:29-22:40)

- Remembered in the Bible for doing more to provoke God's anger than all the kings of Israel before him (1 Kings 16:33)
- Seventh king of Israel's Northern Kingdom
- Inherited the throne from his father Omri
- Reigned for 22 years
- Enjoyed some military success and demonstrated political saavy by marrying Jezebel, a Phoenician princess
- Was led astray by his pagan wife Jezebel (1 Kings 21:25)
- Successes were overshadowed by his spiritual compromises and failures (1 Kings 16:30)
- Worshipped idols, as evidenced by building an altar for Baal (1 Kings 16:32)
- Archaeological finds confirm that he built Jezebel an ivory palace (1 Kings 22:39)
- Obeyed Elijah's command to gather the prophets of Baal in the dramatic standoff to see whose sacrifice would be consumed with fire (1 Kings 18:20-40)
- Did not interfere with the execution of the prophets of Baal by the order of Elijah
- Although he ultimately humbled himself before God, the prophecy of his and his descendants' destruction would come true (1 Kings 21:17-22:40)

Baal (Judges 2:10-23)

- Also known as the fertility god

- The god of the Canaanite religion

- Verb tense meaning "to marry or rule over"

- Noun meaning "lord, owner, or husband"

- Not every mention of the word Baal is evil, as it was a personal name for a man (1 Chronicles 5:5, 9:35-36) and the name for certain places (Joshua 11:17, 2 Samuel 6:2)

- Proved to be a great temptation for Israel in worshiping idols (Judges 2:10-23, 2 Kings 17:16)

- Baal-berith was a Canaanite god that the Israelites worshiped after the death of Gideon (Judges 8:33)

- Baal-peor was a Moabite deity that the Israelites worshiped when they had illicit sexual relations with Moabite women (Deuteronomy 4:3, Hosea 9:10)

- Baal-zebob was a Philistine god whom King Ahaziah consulted after injuring himself, which ignited the Lord's indignation against him (2 Kings 1:1-18)

- Jesus was accused of being possessed by Beelzebub, the prince of demons (Mark 3:20-22)

- Jesus used it to describe Satan (Mark 3:23-29)

- Prophet Hosea refused to use the word "baal," meaning my master, as it reminded the Israelites of the false god Baal that they had worshipped (Hosea 2:16-17)

Cain (Genesis 4)

- Personal name meaning "acquisition"
- Firstborn son of Adam and Eve (Genesis 4:1)
- A farmer (4:2)
- Brought an offering from the "fruit of the ground" to the Lord, which God did not accept (4:3)
- Worshiped God selfishly, instead of genuinely as his brother Abel had done (Hebrews 11:4, John 4:23-24)
- Received a warning from God about controlling his anger or it would lead to sin (4:5-7)
- Committed the first murder in the history of the world, killing his brother in a field (4:8)
- Severed his relationship with God when he lacked a repentant heart for his sin (4:9-10)
- Cursed by God, making it difficult for him to reap a harvest (4:11-12)
- Became a wandering beggar (4:12, 14)
- Feared that his punishment from God would lead to his death at the hands of someone seeking revenge (4:13-14)
- Protected by God with a seal warning people not to kill him (4:15)

Haman (Esther 3-7)

- Personal name meaning "magnificent"

- Prime minister under the Persian King Ahasuerus (Esther 3:1)

- Despised Mordecai for not bowing down to him and paying him homage (3:2-5)

- Fierce enemy of the Jews

- Consulted his wife Zeresh on multiple occasions, who may have been more wicked than him (5:10,14, 6:13)

- Devised a plan to annihilate the Jewish population (3:6-15)

- Vowed to pay the king 10,000 talents of silver (several billions of dollars) for permission to carry out his plan (3:9)

- Built gallows to hang Mordecai from for his lack of respect

- Invited to a banquet by Queen Esther, which pleased him for he did not know about her Jewish ancestry (5:1-8, 7:1-2)

- Was commanded by the king to honor Mordecai (for thwarting a plot to assassinate the king) on the day he planned to hang him (3:6-11)

- Plead for his life when he discovered that Esther was Jewish and his plot was exposed (7:3-7)

- Hanged on the gallows that he had made for Mordecai (7:10)

Herod the Great (Matthew 2,14)

- The name Herod was given to the family ruling Palestine just before the first century

- Half Jewish and the son of an Edomite

- Lived from 74 to 4 B.C.

- Felt it necessary to show unwavering support for Augustus, Emperor of Rome, after supporting his opponent Mark Antony

- Able administrator of Palestine, although better known for his greed and insurrection against Roman rulers

- Encountered the wise men from the East who had reported that the King of the Jews had been born (Matthew 2:1-11)

- Lived in fear that a Messiah would become king and assume his throne, so he ordered the massacre of all the infant male children in Bethlehem (Matthew 2:16-18)

- Suspected everyone as a threat to his throne, including family members

- Murdered wives and his own son because he felt threatened by them

- One of the most cruel rulers of all history

- Bribed the Jews by building a lavish temple

- His son, Herod Antipas ordered that John the Baptist be beheaded at the request of the daughter of Herodias (Matthew 14:1-12)

Jezebel (1 Kings 16-21, 2 Kings 9)

- Personal name meaning "where is the prince"

- Wife of King Ahab of Israel (1 Kings 16:31)

- Stirred up the king to do evil (21:25)

- Brought the worship of Baal from Sidon to Israel (1 Kings 16:32)

- Tried to destroy all of the prophets of the Lord (18:4)

- Made the prophets of Baal and Asherah a part of the royal family (18:19)

- Threatened to kill Elijah after he executed the prophets of Baal in the standoff at Mount Carmel (18:20-19:2)

- Devised a plan to have Naboth stoned to death after he refused to sell his vineyard to the king (21:1-16)

- Death was prophesied by Elijah (21:23)

- Influenced her son, Joram, during his reign in Judah

- Tried to seduce Jehu, who was anointed King of Israel by Elisha, after he had Joram assassinated (2 Kings 9:1-26)

- Died violently by being trampled by horses after being thrown out of a window at Jehu's command (2 Kings 9:30-37)

Judas Iscariot (The Gospels, Acts 1:12-25)

- Personal name meaning "praise God"

- Name Isacriot means "man of Kerioth", a town near Hebron

- One of the twelve apostles of Jesus

- Only apostle from Judea

- Listed last of the disciples in each of the gospels because of his betrayal (Matthew 10:3-5)

- Betrayed Jesus for thirty shekels of silver to the Jewish authorities (Matthew 26:14-16)

- Acted as treasurer for the disciples although he was known for being a thief (John 12:5-6)

- Jesus predicted his betrayal at the Last Supper (Luke 22:21)

- Following Jesus' arrest, he attempted to return the pieces of silver (Matthew 27:3-4)

- Wanted to reverse what had been done but could not and used the money to buy a field (Matthew 27:6-10 & Acts 1:18-19)

- Hanged himself from a tree (Matthew 27:5)

- Died with sorrow, but not repentance (Matthew 27:3 & 2 Corinthians 7:10)

Pharaoh, of the Exodus (Exodus 1-14)

- Name meaning "great house" for the ancient kings of Egypt

- Absolute monarch of Egypt

- Dealt harshly with the Israelites as they grew in number, enslaving them out of fear (Exodus 1: 8-14)

- Ordered the killing of the sons of Israel (1:15-16)

- Ordered that every son born be thrown into the river (1:17-22)

- Did not know the Lord (5:2)

- Forced the Israelites to gather their own straw to make bricks after Moses' first request to release them from slavery (5:4-21)

- God hardened his heart (9:12)

- Responsible for bringing ten plagues onto Egypt (7:14-12:30)

- Commander of the Egyptian army (14:4)

- Pursued the Israelites to the Red Sea after letting them go (14:5-9)

- He and his army were destroyed at the crossing of the Red Sea (14:15-31)

Pharisees (The Gospels, Acts)

- Name meaning "the separated ones"
- Separated in three ways: from the people, from themselves (to study the law), and from pagan practices
- Largest and most influential religious/political party during New Testament times
- Viewed the Old Testament as the authoritative word of God
- Taught that the way to God was through obedience to the law
- Opposed Jesus because he would not accept the teachings of the oral law as binding (Mark 7:1-13)
- Established and controlled synagogues (Luke 20:46-47)
- Accused by Jesus of exercising great control over the general population by placing heavy burdens on the people (Matthew 23:1-4)
- Tended to be self-sufficient, hypocritical, and prideful (Luke 18:10-14, Matthew 23:5-36)
- Often looked down on others who were non-Pharisees as unclean (Luke 7:36-50)
- Paul asserted that he was a Pharisee before converting to Christianity (Acts 23:1-10)
- Contributed to the plot to have Jesus killed (Mark 3:6, John 18:3)

Pilate (The Gospels)

- Roman governor of Judea under whom Jesus suffered (1 Timothy 6:13)

- Came to power in A.D. 26

- Served under Emperor Tiberius (Luke 3:1)

- Hatred of the Jews led him to brutally suppress protests by the Jewish people (Luke 13:1)

- Allowed himself to be pressured by Jewish religious leaders who wanted Jesus executed

- Asked Jesus if he was King of the Jews, to which Jesus replied, "You have said it." (Mark 15:2)

- Remained unconvinced that Jesus was any serious threat to political power (John 19:4)

- Convicted Jesus of treason (John 18:28-19:16)

- Released Barabbas at the request of the people and condemned Jesus to be executed (Matthew 27:15-23)

- Ceremonially washed his hands clean of guilt for the crucifixion of an innocent man (Matthew 27:24-26)

- Granted the request of Joseph of Arimathea to take Jesus' body and bury it properly (Matthew 27:57-61)

- United with the Gentiles and the people of Israel against Jesus (Acts 4:27)

Satan (Ezekiel 28, Revelation 20)

- Created by God (Ezekiel 28:12-13)

- Personal being with a very real existence (Job 1:8, 2:1, Matthew 4:1-11)

- Experiences the emotions of fear (James 2:19), pain (Revelation 20:10), and preference (Luke 22:31)

- Demonstrated intellectual ability by memorizing scripture during his temptations of Jesus (Matthew 4:6)

- Arrogance led him to attempt to take the place of God in heaven (Isaiah 14:12-15, 1 Timothy 3:6) after the sixth day of creation and before the fall (Genesis 1:31, Exodus 20:11)

- Cast out of heaven for his pride (Ezekiel 28)

- Deceived Eve in the Garden of Eden leading to the fall of man (Genesis 3:1-6, 2 Corinthians 11:3)

- Limited ability to perform miracles (Exodus 7:12)

- Disguises himself as an angel (2 Corinthians 11:14)

- Sole reason we have need to put on the armor of God each day (Ephesians 6:10-20, 1 Peter 5:8)

- Accuses man of sin before God night and day (Revelation 12:10)

- Day of Judgment for him, the demons, and all those not in Christ is certain (Genesis 3:16, Hebrews 2:14-15, Revelation 12:12-17, Revelation 20)

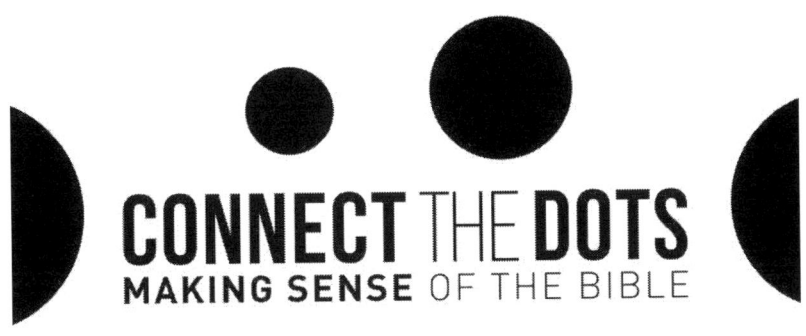

66 Books Summary
OLD TESTAMENT

Scripture is God-Breathed
All Scripture is inspired by God and is useful to teach us what is true and to make us realize what is wrong in our lives. It corrects us when we are wrong and teaches us to do what is right. God uses it to prepare and equip his people to do every good work.
(2 Timothy 3:16-17, NLT)

The Law, the Prophets, and the Writings
Then He said to them, "These are the words which I spoke to you while I was still with you, that all things must be fulfilled which were written in the Law of Moses and the Prophets and the Psalms concerning Me."
(Luke 24:44)

From Beginning to End
So that upon you may fall the guilt of all the righteous blood shed on earth, from the blood of righteous Abel to the blood of Zechariah, the son of Berechiah, whom you murdered between the temple and the altar.
(Matthew 23:35)

Is the Bible Reliable?

Have you ever thought about why you trust the Bible? It claims to be the word of God (2 Timothy 3:16-17), but how do you know that is true? Is it even important to know that it is true? Absolutely! (1 Peter 3:15)

The word of God has been under attack ever since Satan tricked Eve in the Garden. If we can't trust His word as true and reliable as we read it today, then this will have serious implications on our faith and trust in God. Jesus Himself was the Word (John 1:1, 14), so it is important to understand how and why we can trust that the Bible – the word of God – is true.

Jesus Validates the Old Testament as Scripture

Jesus validated the Old Testament as trustworthy when He walked this earth. In Matthew 4, when Jesus was being tempted by Satan, He used the phrase, "It is written," three times (Satan used it once as well). By this, He indicated that what was written had binding effects and was trustworthy.

When appearing to His disciples after the resurrection, Jesus referred to the Law, the prophets, and the writings, which encompass the Jewish Scriptures. In saying this, Jesus expressed the scope of the Old Testament to include the Law of Moses (first five books of the Old Testament), the Prophets (major and minor prophets included in the Old Testament), and the Psalms (which include Song of Solomon, Job, Proverbs, and Ecclesiastes).

One additional verse that is used to show Jesus' regard of the Old Testament scriptures comes from an obscure verse in Matthew 23, where Jesus included the spilling of blood in two separate accounts – one found in Genesis 4 (Cain and Abel) and the other one found in 2 Chronicles 24:20-22 (Zechariah).

Genesis is the first book and 2 Chronicles is the last book of the Hebrew Bible. In essence, Jesus was saying, "From beginning to end." Jesus saw the Old Testament as reliable and trustworthy from beginning to end. If He, being all-knowing and all-powerful can trust the Old Testament writings, so can you.

These are just a few ways to show through the person of Jesus that the Bible is trustworthy and reliable. However, there are many other reasons to trust the Old Testament. Why do you trust the Bible to be true?

Why do you trust the Old Testament to be accurate?

GENESIS

In the beginning, God created the heavens and the earth. (Genesis 1:1, ESV)

PEN — Moses is considered by most to be the author of Genesis.

PEOPLE — Adam and Eve, Noah, Abraham and Sarah, Isaac and Rebekah, Ishmael, Jacob, Esau, Joseph

PERIOD — 1445 - 1400 B.C.

PLACE — Garden of Eden, Canaan, Hebron, Egypt

PURPOSE — Genesis describes God's great love for His creation, man's disobedience and His plan to redeem His creation.

PASSAGES — 1:1, 27; 2:16-17, 24; 3:15; 12:1-3; 50:19-20

EXODUS

> God said to Moses, "I AM WHO I AM. This is what you are to say to the Israelites, I AM has sent me to you'"
> (Exodus 3:14, NIV)

PEN Moses is recognized as the author of Exodus.

PEOPLE Moses, Aaron, Pharoah

PERIOD 1445 - 1400 B.C.

PLACE Egypt, Midian, Sinai

PURPOSE Exodus describes God's fulfillment of His promises to the patriarchs to make their descendants a great nation.

PASSAGES 3:14; 19:5-6; 20:1-17

LEVITICUS

You shall be holy, for I the LORD your God am holy.
(Leviticus 19:2, ESV)

PEN   Moses was the author of Leviticus.

PEOPLE   Moses, Aaron

PERIOD   1445 - 1400 B.C.

PLACE   Sinai

PURPOSE Leviticus describes God's provision of rules and guidelines to govern his people as He called them to live holy lives as a testimony to others of their relationship with Him.

PASSAGES 17:11; 19:2, 18; 20:7-8; 27:30

NUMBERS

Pardon, I pray, the iniquity of this people according to the greatness of Thy loving-kindness,
(Numbers 14:19, NASB)

PEN Moses is considered to have written Numbers.

PEOPLE Moses, Aaron, Joshua, Caleb, Balaam, Eleazar

PERIOD 1445 - 1400 B.C.

PLACE Sinai, Kadesh, Moab

PURPOSE Numbers describes God's faithfulness to bring His chosen people to the promised land, despite their rebellion.

PASSAGES 6:24-26; 13:30; 14:18-19, 22-23; 23:19

DEUTERONOMY

Love the LORD your God with all your heart and with all your soul and with all your strength (Deuteronomy 6:5, NIV)

PEN Moses was the author of Deuteronomy.

PEOPLE Moses, Joshua

PERIOD 1445 - 1400 B.C.

PLACE Moab

PURPOSE Deuteronomy describes the laws of God to the Israelites, as well as the passing of leadership to Joshua and the death of Moses as the Israelites prepared to enter the Promised Land.

PASSAGES 2:7; 4:9, 39-40; 6:4-9

JOSHUA

Choose for yourselves this day whom you will serve...But as for me and my household, we will serve the LORD.
(Joshua 24:15, NIV)

PEN   Joshua was the primary author of the book of Joshua.

PEOPLE   Joshua, Caleb, Eleazar, Rahab

PERIOD   1400 - 1380 B.C.

PLACE   Canaan

PURPOSE   Joshua describes God's fulfillment of His promise to the Israelites to give them the Promised Land.

PASSAGES 1:8-9; 24:15

JUDGES

They abandoned the LORD, the God of their ancestors, (Judges 2:12, NLT)

PEN   Samuel is considered by many to be the author of Judges; however, the author is not specifically identified.

PEOPLE   Othniel, Ehud, Shamgar, Deborah, Barak, Gideon, Abimelech, Tola, Jair, Jepththah, Ibzan, Elon, Abdon, Samson

PERIOD   1050 - 1000 B.C.

PLACE   Canaan

PURPOSE   Judges describes the Israelites' repeated spiral of wickedness and unfaithfulness to God, and God's judging of their sin, in addition to His provision of the judges to lead the Israelites to return to Him.

PASSAGES   2:10, 12; 21:25

But Ruth replied, "Don't urge me to leave you or to turn back from you. Where you go I will go, and where you stay I will stay. Your people will be my people and your God my God." (Ruth 1:16, NIV)

PEN The author of Ruth is unknown, but Samuel is often considered to have written the book.

PEOPLE Ruth, Naomi, Boaz

PERIOD 1010 - 970 B.C.

PLACE Moab, Bethlehem

PURPOSE Ruth describes the kinsman-redeemer relationship that we have in Christ, and reflects the Gentile (non-Jewish) bloodline of Jesus, who came to save all mankind.

PASSAGES 1:16-17; 4:14

1 SAMUEL

For God sees not as man sees, for man looks at the outward appearance, but the LORD looks at the heart. (1 Samuel 16:7, NASB)

PEN   Samuel wrote only a portion of the book of First Samuel. Nathan and Gad also wrote parts of the book.

PEOPLE   Hannah, Eli, Samuel, Saul, Jonathan, David, Goliath, Abigail

PERIOD   970 - 720 B.C.

PLACE   Israel

PURPOSE First Samuel describes the first kings of Israel (Saul and David), their leadership, and their impact on the Israelite nation.

PASSAGES 3:10; 15:22; 16:7; 17:45

2 SAMUEL

Who am I, O Sovereign LORD, and what is my family, that you have brought me this far? (2 Samuel 7:18, NLT)

PEN   Samuel and others such as Nathan and Gad wrote the book of Second Samuel.

PEOPLE   David, Abner, Joab, Nathan, Bathsheba, Uriah, Absalom

PERIOD   970 - 720 B.C.

PLACE   Israel

PURPOSE   Second Samuel describes the reign of King David, his victories, his sins and defeats, and his relationship with God as a "man after God's own heart".

PASSAGES   7:12-13, 16, 18; 12:13; 22:2-4

1 KINGS

But the LORD was not in the wind. After the wind there was an earthquake, but the LORD was not in the earthquake. After the earthquake came a fire, but the LORD was not in the fire. And after the fire came a gentle whisper. (1 Kings 19:11-12, NIV)

PEN Jeremiah is recognized as the author of First Kings.

PEOPLE David, Solomon, Jeroboam, Rehoboam, Abijam, Asa, Ahab, Elijah, Naboth, Jezebel, Jehoshaphat, Ahaziah

PERIOD 550 B.C.

PLACE Israel, Judah

PURPOSE First Kings describes how Israel's kings led the people away from following God and the resulting split of the kingdom and subsequent conquest by pagan nations.

PASSAGES 3:9; 8:27; 9:4-5; 11:11; 19:11-12

2 KINGS

Neither before nor after Josiah was there a king like him who turned to the LORD as he did – with all his heart and with all his soul and with all his strength, (2 Kings 23:25, NIV)

PEN	Jeremiah is recognized as the author of Second Kings
PEOPLE	Elijah, Jehoram, Elisha, Shunammite woman, Naaman, Ahaziah, Jehu, Hezekiah, Josiah
PERIOD	550 B.C.
PLACE	Israel, Judah
PURPOSE	Second Kings describes how Israel's kings led the people away from following God and their subsequent conquest by pagan nations.
PASSAGES	20:5; 22:11; 23:25, 27

1 CHRONICLES

Know the God of your father, and serve him with a whole heart and with a willing mind, for the LORD searches all hearts and understands every plan and thought. (1 Chron. 28:9, ESV)

PEN   Ezra is considered to have written First Chronicles.

PEOPLE   Saul, David, Nathan, Solomon

PERIOD   450 - 425 B.C.

PLACE   Israel

PURPOSE   First Chronicles outlines the history of God's people, the Israelites, from Adam through the reign of King David.

PASSAGES   4:10; 17:11-14; 28:9, 20; 29:17

2 CHRONICLES

If my people who are called by my name humble themselves, and pray and seek my face and turn from their wicked ways, then I will hear from heaven and will forgive their sin and heal their land. (2 Chronicles 7:14, ESV)

PEN   Ezra is recognized as the author of Second Chronicles.

PEOPLE   Solomon, Rehoboam, Abijah, Asa, Jehoshaphat, Jerhoram, Ahaziah, Joash, Amaziah, Uzziah, Jotham, Ahaz, Hezekiah, Manasseh, Amon, Josiah

PERIOD   450 - 425 B.C.

PLACE   Israel, Judah, Babylon

PURPOSE   Second Chronicles recounts the history of the Israelites from Solomon's reign, through the Babylonian captivity and return of the exiles to Jerusalem.

PASSAGES   7:14; 16:9; 20:15; 32:7-8

> For Ezra had set his heart to study the law of the LORD, and to practice it, and to teach his statutes and ordinances in Israel. (Ezra 7:10, NASB)

PEN Ezra wrote the book of Ezra.

PEOPLE Cyrus, Darius, Ezra, Artaxerxes, Zerubbabel, Jeshua, Haggai, Zechariah

PERIOD 456 - 444 B.C.

PLACE Jerusalem

PURPOSE Ezra describes the fulfillment of God's promise to return the Israelites to the Promised Land after 70 years of Babylonian captivity, and the Israelites' rebuilding of the temple in Jerusalem and rededication of the people.

PASSAGES 1:3; 7:10

NEHEMIAH

LORD, let your ear be attentive to the prayer of this your servant and to the prayer of your servants who delight in revering your name.
(Nehemiah 1:11, NIV)

PEN	Ezra is considered to be the author of Nehemiah.
PEOPLE	Nehemiah, Artaxerxes, Sanballat, Tobiah, Ezra
PERIOD	456 - 444 B.C.
PLACE	Babylon, Jerusalem
PURPOSE	Nehemiah describes the return of the Israelites from captivity in Babylon and the rebuilding of the walls of Jerusalem.
PASSAGES	1:11; 2:20; 6:15-16

ESTHER

And who knows but that you have come to your royal position for such a time as this?
(Esther 4:14, NIV)

PEN	It is uncertain who wrote the book of Esther, but many believe that Mordecai was the author.
PEOPLE	Ahasuerus (Xerxes), Esther, Mordecai, Haman
PERIOD	465 B.C.
PLACE	Susa (in Persia)
PURPOSE	Esther describes God's sovereignty and provision, and how He uses His faithful servants to accomplish His purposes.
PASSAGES	4:14

JOB

Stop and consider the wondrous works of God.
(Job 37:14, ESV)

PEN The author of Job is unknown.

PEOPLE Job, Eliphaz, Bildad, Zophar, Elihu

PERIOD Date unknown, possibly during the time of the patriarchs (2000 – 1500 B.C.)

PLACE Uz

PURPOSE Job demonstrates that suffering is not an indication of God's judgment on a person's life or faith, and shows the need for man to recognize God's sovereignty.

PASSAGES 1:8; 19:25; 23:10; 28:28; 37:14; 38:4-7

PSALMS

Let the words of my mouth and the meditation of my heart be acceptable in your sight, O LORD, my rock and my redeemer. (Psalm 19:14,ESV)

PEN Although King David wrote 73 of the psalms, many other writers, including Solomon and Moses, contributed individual psalms.

PEOPLE David, Solomon, sons of Korah, Asaph, Heman, Ethan, Moses

PERIOD Various dates; final psalm composed 400 B.C.

PLACE As varied as the authors who composed the psalms

PURPOSE Psalms expresses praise and worship and dependence on God, His love and provision, and His Word in our lives.

PASSAGES 1:1-3; 8:4-5, 9; 19:14; 22:18; 23:1-6; 24:1; 33:12; 37:4; 42:1; 46:1, 10; 51:10-12, 16-17; 56:3; 86:15; 91:1, 4; 100:1-5; 103:12; 119:11, 105; 121:1-2; 139:13-17, 23-24

PROVERBS

The fear of the LORD is the beginning of knowledge;
(Proverbs 1:7, ESV)

PEN	The majority of Proverbs was written by Solomon; brief sections were written by Agur and King Lemuel.
PEOPLE	Solomon, Agur, Lemuel
PERIOD	950 - 700 B.C.
PLACE	Israel
PURPOSE	Proverbs provides wisdom for godly living, addressing every aspect of our lives.
PASSAGES	1:7; 3:5-6; 15:1; 16:18; 22:6; 31:10, 28-30

ECCLESIASTES

For everything there is a season, and a time for every matter under heaven: (Eccl. 3:1, ESV)

PEN   Solomon wrote the book of Ecclesiastes.

PEOPLE   Solomon

PERIOD   935 B.C.

PLACE   Israel

PURPOSE Ecclesiastes conveys that only in living in obedience to God will we find meaning and satisfaction in life.

PASSAGES 1:2; 3:1-8; 4:9-12; 12:1, 13-14

SONG OF SOLOMON

Many waters cannot quench love, nor will rivers overflow it; (Song of Solomon 8:7, NASB)

PEN   Solomon wrote the Song of Solomon.

PEOPLE   Solomon, Shulamite, daughters of Jerusalem

PERIOD   971 - 931 B.C.

PLACE   Jerusalem and southeast of the Sea of Galilee

PURPOSE   Song of Solomon describes not only the richness of the relationship of a man and wife fully committed to each other, but also reflects God's love for His people.

PASSAGES 7:10; 8:6-7

ISAIAH

But those who trust in the LORD will renew their strength; they will soar on wings like eagles; they will run and not grow weary; they will walk and not faint. (Isaiah 40:31, HCSB)

PEN   The prophet Isaiah wrote the book of Isaiah.

PEOPLE   Isaiah, Hezekiah

PERIOD   740 - 680 B.C.

PLACE   Judah

PURPOSE   Isaiah describes the call for the Israelites to return to faithfulness to God, and it prophesies of the life and death of the coming Messiah.

PASSAGES   1:18; 6:3, 5, 8; 7:14; 9:6; 26:3; 28:16; 30:15; 40:8, 28-31; 41:10; 43:1-2; 49:15-16; 53:1-9; 55:8-9, 11-12; 59:1-2; 61:1

JEREMIAH

For I know the plans I have for you,'" says the LORD. "'They are plans for good and not for disaster, to give you a future and a hope.
(Jeremiah 29:11,NLT)

PEN The prophet Jeremiah wrote the book of Jeremiah.

PEOPLE Jeremiah, Josiah, Jehoiakim, Baruch, Nebuchadnezzar, Zedekiah

PERIOD 627 - 585 B.C.

PLACE Jerusalem, Egypt

PURPOSE Jeremiah describes how sins have consequences, yet God remains faithful to redeem and restore His people who return to Him.

PASSAGES 1:5; 9:23-24; 17:7-8; 29:11-13; 31:3, 31-33; 32:27; 33:3

LAMENTATIONS

The LORD's loving kindness indeed never ceases, for his compassions never fail. They are new every morning; Great is your faithfulness. (Lam. 3:22-23, NASB)

PEN Jeremiah is recognized as the author of Lamentations.

PEOPLE Jeremiah, Zedekiah

PERIOD 585 B.C.

PLACE Jerusalem (written while in exile in Egypt)

PURPOSE Lamentations describes the trouble and sorrow that the Israelites endured as a result of their turning away from God, and expresses how to maintain faith in God during times of tribulation.

PASSAGES 3:22-23

> And I will put my Spirit within you and cause you to walk in my statutes, and you will be careful to observe my ordinances.
> (Ezekiel 36:27, NASB)

PEN   The prophet Ezekiel wrote the book of Ezekiel.

PEOPLE   Ezekiel

PERIOD   592 – 570 B.C.

PLACE   Jerusalem, Judah (written while in exile in Babylon)

PURPOSE Ezekiel describes the sinfulness that led to God's judgment of the Israelites, yet reminds us of His faithfulness to restore His people.

PASSAGES 36:24-28

DANIEL

Until you acknowledge that the Most High is ruler over the kingdom of men, and he gives it to anyone he wants. (Daniel 4:25, HCSB)

PEN   The prophet Daniel wrote the book of Daniel.

PEOPLE   Nebuchadnezzar, Daniel, Shadrach, Meshach, Abednego, Belshazzar, Darius

PERIOD   530 B.C.

PLACE   Babylon

PURPOSE   Daniel describes the faithfulness of Daniel and his friends while in captivity in a foreign land and their impact on the pagan society around them, as well as prophesying about the fall of Babylon and the coming of the promised Messiah.

PASSAGES   2:44; 3:16-18; 4:25; 6:16

HOSEA

For I desire mercy and not sacrifice, and the knowledge of God more than burnt offerings.
(Hosea 6:6, NKJV)

PEN The prophet Hosea wrote the book of Hosea.

PEOPLE Hosea, Gomer

PERIOD 715 – 710 B.C.

PLACE Israel, Judah

PURPOSE Hosea describes the sins of the Israelites, the certainty of judgment, and God's steadfast love and faithfulness.

PASSAGES 6:6; 13:14; 14:9

Return to the LORD your God, for he is merciful and compassionate, slow to get angry and filled with unfailing love. He is eager to relent and not punish.
(Joel 2:13, NLT)

PEN   The prophet Joel wrote the book of Joel.

PEOPLE   Joel

PERIOD   Date unknown, possibly 900 – 500 B.C.

PLACE   Judah

PURPOSE   Joel describes the need for true repentance from sin in light of the coming judgment.

PASSAGES   1:15; 2:13, 28-29, 32

AMOS

Seek the LORD that you may live. (Amos 5:6, NASB)

PEN	Amos, a sheepherder, wrote the book of Amos
PEOPLE	Amos
PERIOD	750 B.C.
PLACE	Israel, Judah
PURPOSE	Amos describes the material prosperity, social evils, and pagan worship of the Israelites' and the prophecy of God's coming judgment if the people did not repent.
PASSAGES	3:2; 4:13; 5:6, 24; 7:8; 8:11-12; 9:11

OBADIAH

As you have done, it will be done to you; your deeds will return upon your own head. (Obadiah 1:15, NIV)

PEN   The prophet Obadiah wrote the book of Obadiah.

PEOPLE   Obadiah

PERIOD   586 – 553 B.C.

PLACE   Edom

PURPOSE Obadiah describes God's judgment on the Edomites (descendants of Esau) for attacking the Judeans rather than assisting them when they were under attack from Babylon.

PASSAGES 1:15

JONAH

In my distress I called to the LORD, and he answered me. (Jonah 2:2, NIV)

PEN	The prophet Jonah wrote the book of Jonah.
PEOPLE	Jonah
PERIOD	780 – 760 B.C.
PLACE	Ninevah
PURPOSE	Jonah describes God's love for all people, not just the Israelites, and His desire that everyone should repent of their sins and enter into relationship with Him.
PASSAGES	2:2; 4:2, 11

MICAH

And what does the LORD require of you? To act justly and to love mercy and to walk humbly with your God. (Micah 6:8, NIV)

PEN   The prophet Micah wrote the book of Micah.

PEOPLE   Micah

PERIOD   700 B.C.

PLACE   Judah

PURPOSE Micah describes the corruption and idolatry of the religious and political leadership, leading the people to disregard God, and warns the people of God's coming judgment.

PASSAGES 4:3; 5:2; 6:8; 7:7, 18

NAHUM

The LORD is good, a refuge in times of trouble. He cares for those who trust in him. (Nahum 1:7, NIV)

PEN   The prophet Nahum wrote the book of Nahum.

PEOPLE   Nahum

PERIOD   650 B.C.

PLACE   Ninevah

PURPOSE   Nahum describes how faithfulness to God must be taught and passed down to the next generations. Although the Ninevites had repented and turned to God in Jonah's time, they had not passed the faith to their children, who faced God's impending judgment as a result of their wickedness.

PASSAGES   1:7

HABAKKUK

But the LORD is in his holy temple. Let all the earth be silent before him. (Habakkuk 2:20, NLT)

PEN The prophet Habakkuk wrote the book of Habakkuk.

PEOPLE Habakkuk

PERIOD 610 B.C.

PLACE Judah

PURPOSE Habakkuk reflects the difference between doubting God and not understanding God, and shows that God does not mind our tough questions. When we don't understand, we trust Him.

PASSAGES 2:3-4, 20; 3:18-19

ZEPHANIAH

The LORD your God is in your midst, a mighty one who will save; he will rejoice over you with gladness; he will quiet you by his love; he will exult over you with loud singing.
(Zephaniah 3:17, ESV)

PEN	The prophet Zephaniah wrote the book of Zephaniah.
PEOPLE	Zephaniah
PERIOD	625 B.C.
PLACE	Judah
PURPOSE	Zephaniah calls God's people to repentance, and warns of coming judgment, not only against the sinful Israelites, but the pagan nations around them.
PASSAGES	2:3; 3:17

HAGGAI

"And I will fill this house with glory," says the LORD Almighty. "The silver is mine, and the gold is mine," declares the LORD Almighty. (Haggai 2:7, NIV)

PEN The prophet Haggai wrote the book of Haggai.

PEOPLE Haggai, Zerubbabel, Joshua

PERIOD 520 B.C.

PLACE Jerusalem

PURPOSE Haggai describes the call to God's people to rebuild His temple.

PASSAGES 2:7

ZECHARIAH

"Not by might nor by power, but by my Spirit," says the LORD Almighty. (Zechariah 4:6, NIV)

PEN	The prophet Zechariah wrote the book of Zechariah.
PEOPLE	Zechariah
PERIOD	520 B.C.
PLACE	Jerusalem
PURPOSE	Zechariah describes the call to God's people to finish rebuilding the temple and the admonishment to repent and return to God with all their hearts in order that His promises to them would be fulfilled.
PASSAGES	4:6; 9:9; 12:10

MALACHI

"Bring the full tithe into the storehouse, that there may be food in my house. And thereby put me to the test," says the LORD of hosts, "if I will not open the windows of heaven for you and pour down for you a blessing until there is no more need." (Malachi 3:10,ESV)

PEN   The prophet Malachi wrote the book of Malachi.

PEOPLE   Malachi

PERIOD   450 - 420 B.C.

PLACE   Jerusalem

PURPOSE   Malachi describes how God is unable to bless His people when they are spiritually apathetic. He calls His people to live lives fully committed to Him.

PASSAGES   1:6; 3:6, 8-10

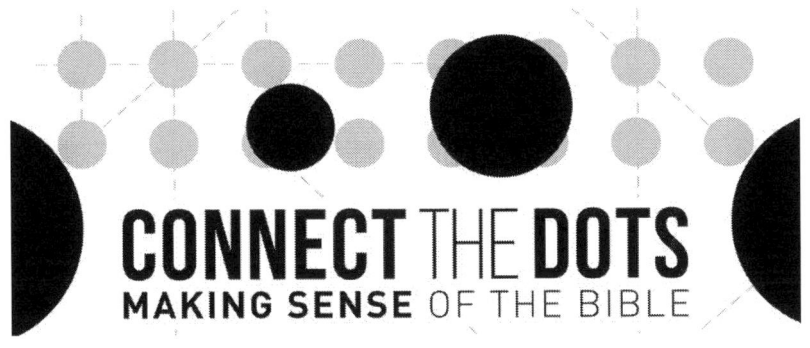

66 Books Summary
NEW TESTAMENT

The Role of the Holy Spirit
These things I have spoken to you while I am still with you. But the Helper, the Holy Spirit, whom the Father will send in my name, he will teach you all things and bring to your remembrance all that I have said to you.
(John 14:25-26)

Peter Validates Paul's Writings
And count the patience of our Lord as salvation, just as our beloved brother Paul also wrote to you according to the wisdom given him, as he does in all his letters when he speaks in them of these matters. There are some things in them that are hard to understand, which the ignorant and unstable twist to their own destruction, as they do the other Scriptures.
(2 Peter 3:15-16)

Validation of the New Testament as Scripture

John 13 begins the last week of Jesus' earthly life. He had just finished washing the disciples' feet and predicted Peter's denial, when He addressed the troubled hearts of His disciples. In their confusion, Jesus promised them the Holy Spirit, who would *teach* them and would *bring to remembrance* all that Jesus said to them (John 14:25-26).

The disciples remembered the events of Jesus' ministry and their implications by the power of the Helper, the Holy Spirit. Jesus validated what they would eventually write down in the books of the New Testament as the Word of God.

The Writings of Paul

But what about Paul? He was not a disciple. In fact, he persecuted early Christians, and gave approval to the stoning of Stephen (Acts 7:58). This is an important question as Paul authored almost half of the New Testament books.

The answer is in 2 Peter 3:16. In this verse, Peter revealed his view of the writings of Paul. He stated, "*There are some things in them that are hard to understand, which the ignorant and unstable twist to their own destruction, as they do the other Scriptures.*" Peter viewed Paul's letters as equal to the writings of the disciples and the Old Testament as he labeled them along with the *other Scriptures*.

The bottom line about the trustworthiness of the Bible is: If God cared enough to have a book written about the way to be restored to a right relationship with Him – like it was in the Garden of Eden – then it would also be reasonable to conclude that He would preserve that book.

This is a simplified way to have confidence in the Bible as you depend on God's word for direction in your life. On the next page, write other reasons to trust the reliability of the Bible, specifically the New Testament.

For further study, visit: **http://www.alwaysbeready.com/bible-evidence**

MATTHEW

Therefore go and make disciples of all nations, baptizing them in the name of the Father and of the Son and of the Holy Spirit, and teaching them to obey everything I have commanded you. And surely I am with you always, to the very end of the age. (Matthew 28:19-20,NIV)

PEN The apostle Matthew wrote the book of Matthew.

PEOPLE Mary, Joseph, Jesus, Herod, John the Baptist, Peter, James, John, Pharisees, Sadducees, Judas, Pilate

PERIOD 55 – 65 A.D.

PLACE Judea, Galilee

PURPOSE Matthew describes how Jesus is the Messiah promised in the Old Testament to the Jews and explains His kingdom as a heavenly, rather than an earthly, one.

PASSAGES 3:17; 5:3-12; 6:9-13, 19-21, 25-26, 33-34; 7:7-8, 12-14; 11:28-30; 18:20; 20:26-28; 22:37-39; 25:35-40; 27:46; 28:18-20

MARK

Then Jesus said to them, "Follow me, and I will make you become fishers of men." (Mark 1:17, NIV)

PEN Mark wrote the book of Mark, based on input and recounting of events from the apostle Peter.

PEOPLE Jesus, John the Baptist, Peter, James, John, Pharisees

PERIOD 55 – 65 A.D.

PLACE Judea, Galilee

PURPOSE Mark describes Jesus' earthly ministry and what He did, primarily to Gentile (non-Jewish) readers. This gospel emphasizes Jesus' actions more than what He said.

PASSAGES 1:17; 2:17; 8:34-37; 10:14-15, 43-45; 12:30-31; 14:36; 15:34; 16:6-7

LUKE

And she gave birth to her first-born son; and she wrapped him in cloths, and laid him in a manger, because there was no room for them in the inn. (Luke 2:7, NASB)

PEN Luke, a Gentile doctor, wrote the book of Luke.

PEOPLE Zacharias, Elizabeth, Mary, Jesus, John the Baptist, Peter, James, John, Pharisees, Pilate

PERIOD 60 A.D.

PLACE Judea, Galilee

PURPOSE Luke provides detailed accounts of Jesus' life and ministry, particularly to give Gentiles (non-Jews) an understanding of Jewish customs and the One who came to be Savior for everyone in the world.

PASSAGES 1:37-38; 2:1-20, 52; 5:31-32; 6:38; 9:23; 15:10; 19:10; 22:15-20, 42; 23:42-43; 24:6

JOHN

For God so loved the world, that he gave his only Son, that whoever believes in him should not perish but have eternal life. (John 3:16, ESV)

PEN The apostle John wrote the book of John.

PEOPLE John the Baptist, Jesus, Peter, James, John, Pharisees, Nicodemus, Samaritan Woman, Martha, Mary, Lazarus, Pilate

PERIOD 80 – 90 A.D.

PLACE Judea, Galilee

PURPOSE John describes the deity and mission of Jesus and the meaning of faith in Him.

PASSAGES 1:1-5, 11-14: 3:3, 16; 6:51; 8:12, 32; 10:10, 27-30; 11:25-26; 13:34-35; 14:1-6, 27; 15:13; 19:26-27; 20:11-18, 30-31; 21:15-17

ACTS

But you will receive power when the Holy Spirit comes on you; and you will be my witnesses in Jerusalem, and in all Judea and Samaria, and to the ends of the earth. (Acts 1:8, NIV)

PEN　　　　Luke, a Gentile doctor, wrote Acts.

PEOPLE　　Jesus, Peter, Stephen, Philip, Barnabas, Paul, James

PERIOD　　61 A.D.

PLACE　　Judea, Samaria, Galatia, Antioch, Ephesus, Corinth, Macedonia, Rome

PURPOSE　Acts describes the spread of the good news of Jesus Christ throughout the world, to Jews and to Gentiles.

PASSAGES　1:8; 2:42-47; 3:19; 4:12; 9:3-8; 16:31

ROMANS

For the wages of sin is death, but the gift of God is eternal life in Christ Jesus our Lord. (Romans 6:23, NIV)

PEN Paul wrote Romans, which was a letter to the Christians in Rome.

PEOPLE Paul, Christians in the church in Rome

PERIOD 57 – 58 A.D.

PLACE Rome (written from Corinth)

PURPOSE Romans provides a systematic explanation of the Christian faith and its application in the day-to-day lives of believers.

PASSAGES 1:16-23; 3:10-11, 23; 5:1, 3-8; 6:23; 8:1, 28-31, 35-39; 10:9-10; 11:33; 12:1-2

1 CORINTHIANS

So whether you eat or drink or whatever you do, do it all for the glory of God. (1 Cor. 10:31, NIV)

PEN   Paul wrote First Corinthians, which was a letter to the Christians in Corinth.

PEOPLE   Paul, Christians in the church in Corinth

PERIOD   55 – 56 A.D.

PLACE   Corinth (written from Ephesus)

PURPOSE   First Corinthians teaches Christian doctrine and behavior, corrects spiritual and moral problems, and answers questions about the faith which caused confusion and division in the church.

PASSAGES   2:14 – 3:3, 11, 16; 6:19-20; 9:24; 10:12-13, 31; 11:23-28; 12:13; 13:1-13; 15:51-57

2 CORINTHIANS

But we *have this treasure in jars of clay to show that this all-surpassing power is from God and not from us.* (2 Cor. 4:7, NIV)

PEN Paul wrote Second Corinthians, which was another letter to the Christians in Corinth.

PEOPLE Paul, Christians in the church in Corinth

PERIOD 56 – 57 A.D.

PLACE Corinth (written from Macedonia)

PURPOSE Second Corinthians addresses the rebellious spirit and lack of respect of the Corinthian Christians and defends Paul's authority as an apostle.

PASSAGES 1:4; 4:7-10, 16-18; 5:7, 17-21; 9:7-8; 10:5; 12:9-10; 13:5

GALATIANS

But the fruit of the Spirit is love, joy, peace, patience, kindness, goodness, faithfulness, gentleness, self-control;
(Galatians 5:22-23,NASB)

PEN	Paul wrote Galatians, which was a letter to the Christians in Galatia.
PEOPLE	Paul, Christians in the church in Galatia
PERIOD	50 – 55 A.D.
PLACE	Galatia (likely written from Antioch, Ephesus or Macedonia)
PURPOSE	Galatians explains that the only way that man can have a relationship with God is through faith in the salvation He provides through Jesus Christ – it cannot be earned through works or adherence to the law.
PASSAGES	2:16, 20-21; 5:13, 16, 22-23; 6:7-9, 14

EPHESIANS

> *Put on the full armor of God, that you may be able to stand firm against the schemes of the devil.* (Ephesians 6:11, NASB)

PEN   Paul wrote Ephesians, which was a letter to the Christians in Ephesus.

PEOPLE   Paul, Christians in the church in Ephesus

PERIOD   60 – 61 A.D.

PLACE   Ephesus (written from Rome)

PURPOSE   Ephesians describes what God has done for us (chapters 1-3), as well as what God expects from us (chapters 4-6).

PASSAGES   1:3-5, 11-14; 2:8-10; 3:14-20; 4:1-2, 11-12, 26-27, 29-32; 5:8, 22-33; 6:1, 11-17

PHILIPPIANS

Don't worry about anything; instead, pray about everything. Tell God what you need, and thank him for what he has done. (Philippians 4:6, NLT)

PEN Paul wrote Philippians, which was a letter to the Christians in Philippi.

PEOPLE Paul, Christians in the church in Philippi

PERIOD 61 A.D.

PLACE Philippi (likely written from Rome)

PURPOSE Philippians thanks the church for their financial and prayerful support for Paul in his ministry and imprisonment and addresses problems in the church, encouraging believers to show the same attitudes of humility, sacrifice and obedience as Christ displayed.

PASSAGES 1:6, 21, 27; 2:3-11, 13-15; 3:7-8, 12-14; 4:4-13

COLOSSIANS

Set your minds on things above, not on earthly things.
(Colossians 3:2, NIV)

PEN	Paul wrote Colossians, which was a letter to the Christians in Colossae.
PEOPLE	Paul, Christians in the church in Colossae
PERIOD	61 A.D.
PLACE	Colossae (written from Rome)
PURPOSE	Colossians emphasizes the supremacy and all-sufficiency of Christ – any practice, person or thing that adds to or detracts from this is false and is not of the faith.
PASSAGES	1:9-10, 28-29; 2:8-10; 3:1-2, 15-17, 23; 4:6

1 THESSALONIANS

Always be joyful. Pray continually, and give thanks whatever happens. That is what God wants for you in Christ Jesus. (1 Thess. 5:16-18, NCV)

PEN	Paul wrote First Thessalonians, which was a letter to the Christians in Thessalonica.
PEOPLE	Paul, Timothy, Silas, Christians in the church in Thessalonica
PERIOD	50 A.D.
PLACE	Thessalonica (written from Corinth)
PURPOSE	First Thessalonians encourages new believers to grow in their relationship with Christ and to not revert to pagan practices and beliefs, answers their questions, and addresses problems in the church.
PASSAGES	2:12; 4:13-18; 5:2, 9-10, 15-19

2 THESSALONIANS

But the Lord is faithful, and he will strengthen you and protect you from the evil one. (2 Thess. 3:3, NET)

PEN	Paul wrote Second Thessalonians, which was another letter to the Christians in Thessalonica.
PEOPLE	Paul, Timothy, Silas, Christians in the church in Thessalonica
PERIOD	51 A.D.
PLACE	Thessalonica (written from Corinth)
PURPOSE	Second Thessalonians admonishes those who believed that the end of the world was imminent to correct their false belief and tells believers not to be idle.
PASSAGES	2:16-17; 3:3

1 TIMOTHY

Fight the good fight of the faith. Take hold of the eternal life to which you were called when you made your good confession in the presence of many witnesses. (1 Timothy 6:12, NIV)

PEN Paul wrote First Timothy, which was a letter to his disciple, Timothy.

PEOPLE Paul, Timothy

PERIOD 63 A.D.

PLACE Ephesus (written from Macedonia)

PURPOSE First Timothy provides instruction regarding care of the church body, appropriate behavior in the church, and qualifications for ministers and those serving in positions in the church.

PASSAGES 1:15; 2:1-2, 5; 3:1-15; 4:12; 5:22; 6:3-5, 7, 10-12

2 TIMOTHY

I know whom I have believed, and am convinced that he is able to guard what I have entrusted to him until that day.
(2 Timothy 1:12, NIV)

PEN	Paul wrote Second Timothy, which was his last letter to his disciple, Timothy.
PEOPLE	Paul, Timothy
PERIOD	66 A.D.
PLACE	Ephesus (written from Rome)
PURPOSE	Second Timothy admonishes Christians to stay true to the inspired Word of God and not be led astray by various teachers and teachings that are not consistent with God's Word.
PASSAGES	1:7, 12; 2:11-13, 15, 22; 3:1, 16-17; 4:1-2, 7-8, 21

TITUS

For the grace of God has appeared that offers salvation to all people. It teaches us to say "no" to ungodliness and worldly passions, and to live self-controlled, upright and godly lives in this present age. (Titus 2:11-12,NIV)

PEN Paul wrote Titus, which was a letter to his disciple, Titus.

PEOPLE Paul, Titus

PERIOD 63 – 65 A.D.

PLACE Crete (written from Macedonia or Nicopolis)

PURPOSE Titus emphasizes the importance of sound doctrine as the foundation for a Christian's life.

PASSAGES 1:6-9; 3:3-8, 11-12; 3:1-2, 5

PHILEMON

I thank my God always, making mention of you in my prayers,
(Philemon 4, NASB)

PEN   Paul wrote Philemon.

PEOPLE   Paul, Onesimus, Philemon

PERIOD   61 A.D.

PLACE   Colossae (written from Rome)

PURPOSE   Philemon reflects that the way that Christians treat others, especially fellow Christians and those of lesser social or economic status, should be a reflection of Christ's love for every person.

PASSAGES   1:4-6

HEBREWS

Let us hold unswervingly to the hope we profess, for he who promised is faithful. (Hebrews 10:23, NIV)

PEN It is uncertain who wrote the book of Hebrews.

PEOPLE The unknown author, Hebrew (Jewish) Christians

PERIOD 64 – 68 A.D.

PLACE Unknown, although references indicate the location was likely Italy

PURPOSE Hebrews admonishes Christians to hold firm to their faith in Christ, and details how Jesus was superior in person and priesthood than all of the Old Testament patriarchs and leaders on whom the Jews had previously based their standing with God.

PASSAGES 2:1, 18; 3:12-14; 4:12, 14-16; 6:19; 7:25-26; 9:22, 27; 10:23-25, 32-39; 11:1, 6; 12:1-3, 5-6, 11; 13:5, 8, 15-16

JAMES

Religion that God our Father accepts as pure and faultless is this: to look after orphans and widows in their distress and to keep oneself from being polluted by the world. (James 1:27,NIV)

PEN	James, the half-brother of Jesus, is recognized has having written the book of James
PEOPLE	James, all Christians scattered throughout the world
PERIOD	45 – 50 A.D.
PLACE	Christian churches throughout the Mediterranean region outside of Palestine (written from Jerusalem)
PURPOSE	James provides practical instruction regarding how Christians should conduct themselves, with faith and hearing translating into obedience, love and action.
PASSAGES	1:2-3, 5, 13-15, 17, 22, 27; 2:14-19, 24, 26; 3:1, 5, 17; 4:7-8, 10; 5:12, 16

1 PETER

Cast all your anxiety on him because he cares for you. (1 Peter 5:7, NIV)

PEN   The apostle Peter wrote the book of First Peter.

PEOPLE   Peter, Gentile (primarily) Christians scattered throughout the world

PERIOD   63 – 64 A.D.

PLACE   Roman provinces in Asia Minor (written from Rome)

PURPOSE   First Peter encourages believers to stay strong in their faith, even when facing persecution and suffering, and to reflect God's love to their persecutors.

PASSAGES   1:4, 6-8, 14-16; 2:4-5, 9, 16, 21-24; 3:1-4, 7-9, 15; 4:13, 16; 5:6-8

2 PETER

The Lord is not slow to fulfill his promise as some count slowness, but is patient toward you, not wishing that any should perish, but that all should reach repentance. (1 Peter 3:9, ESV)

PEN	The apostle Peter wrote the book of Second Peter.
PEOPLE	Peter, Gentile (primarily) Christians scattered throughout the world
PERIOD	66 – 67 A.D.
PLACE	Roman provinces in Asia Minor (written from Rome)
PURPOSE	Second Peter urges believers to stand firm in the truth of the gospel in the face of false teachings.
PASSAGES	1:5-8, 16, 20-21; 3:8-11

1 JOHN

If we confess our sins, he is faithful and just to forgive us our sins and to cleanse us from all unrighteousness. (1 John 1: 9, ESV)

PEN The apostle John wrote the book of First John.

PEOPLE John, Christians throughout Asia Minor

PERIOD 90 A.D.

PLACE Roman provinces in Asia Minor (written from Ephesus)

PURPOSE First John expresses that any teaching or doctrine that adds to, or takes away from, salvation through Jesus' life, death and resurrection, is false and must be rejected.

PASSAGES 1:9; 2:1, 6, 15-17; 3:1-3, 16, 18; 4:1-11, 15, 18-19; 5:11-15

2 JOHN

And this is love: that we walk in obedience to his commands. As you have heard from the beginning, his command is that you walk in love. (2 John 1:6, NIV)

PEN	The apostle John wrote the book of Second John.
PEOPLE	John, Christians in an unspecified church in Asia Minor
PERIOD	80 – 90 A.D.
PLACE	Asia Minor (written from Ephesus)
PURPOSE	Second John exhorts Christians to live and act in obedience to Jesus' commandments.
PASSAGES	1:6

3 JOHN

Beloved, do not imitate evil but imitate good. Whoever does good is from God; whoever does evil has not seen God. (3 John 1:11, ESV)

PEN   The apostle John wrote the book of Third John.

PEOPLE   John, Gaius, Diotrephes, Demetrius

PERIOD   80 – 90 A.D.

PLACE   Asia Minor (written from Ephesus)

PURPOSE Third John admonishes Christians to put the needs of others above their own personal desires.

PASSAGES 1:4, 11

Urging you to defend the faith that God has entrusted once for all time to his holy people. (Jude 1:3, NLT)

PEN   Jude, a half-brother of Jesus, wrote the book of Jude.

PEOPLE   Jude, Christians in unspecified churches in Asia Minor

PERIOD   70 – 80 A.D.

PLACE   Asia Minor (likely written from Jerusalem)

PURPOSE   Jude admonishes Christians to stand firm in the faith, resisting false teachings that encourage moral decadence while claiming spiritual superiority.

PASSAGES   1:3-4, 24-25

REVELATION

Behold, I stand at the door and knock. If anyone hears my voice and opens the door, I will come in to him and dine with him, and he with me. (Revelation 3:20, NKJV)

PEN — The apostle John wrote Revelation

PEOPLE — John, Jesus, Christians in churches in Asia Minor (Ephesus, Smyrna, Pergamum, Thyatira, Sardis, Philadelphia, Laodicea)

PERIOD — 95 A.D.

PLACE — Asia Minor (Ephesus, Smyrna, Pergamum, Thyatira, Sardis, Philadelphia, Laodicea) (written from Patmos)

PURPOSE — Revelation addresses problems in the churches and depicts the end of time, with the return of Christ in all His glory, the judgment that each person will face, and the eternal worship and glorification of God.

PASSAGES — 1:8; 2:4, 10; 3:15-16, 18, 20; 4:11; 12:11; 19:11-15; 20:11-15; 21:3-4; 22:18-20

50 Day Reading Plan
Yield Some Time to God

Reading Plan

This reading plan is designed to take you through the Bible (from Genesis to Revelation) in less than fifty days! I know that is an aggressive goal, but our aim is not to bore into all the details of these stories, but to get an overarching view of the Bible as a whole.

As you read, you will begin connecting the dots, understanding how individual stories and characters fit together to tell the bigger story of God's plan to redeem mankind. To assist you with this process, we have included portions of the Bible to scan and daily readings for each week.

Weekly Scanning

For the next 50 days, you will walk through – or should I say run through – the entire Bible. Each week, there are assigned portions of the Bible to scan. Skim these chapters or books in one sitting. Do not read these word for word, but instead, allow the Holy Spirit to draw your attention to areas on which He wants you to focus. Make a note about areas of particular interest that you can refer to at a later time for further study.

Daily Reading

In addition to the weekly scanning, you have daily readings that should take less than 30 minutes and are designed to be read in one sitting. Read the assigned chapters for each day, but do not spend a great deal of time studying the material. Again, make notes about areas of particular interest that you can refer to at a later time for further study.

Moms & Dads

If you are a parent of younger children, we encourage you to use the readings associated with each day, as well as using the *Jesus Storybook Bible* written by Sally Lloyd-Jones. Discuss the readings each week with your children. Use the Inductive Bible Study approach as a guide to help you ask questions that draw information from them.

We pray this gives your family an understanding of the Bible in a new way as you experience 50 days through the Bible together.

Questions to Consider

1. **Observe.** What does it say?
    a. Who did you read about?
    b. What happened?
    c. Where did it happen?
    d. How did they feel, respond, act...?

2. **Interpret.** What does it mean?
    a. What did God want you to learn by this?
    b. What was the author trying to communicate?

3. **Apply.** What does it mean for (not to) you?
    a. How does this apply to your life?
    b. What one new truth did you learn?

Commit yourselves wholeheartedly to these commands that I am giving you today. Repeat them again and again to your children. Talk about them when you are at home and when you are on the road, when you are going to bed and when you are getting up... Write them on the doorposts of your house...
(Deuteronomy 6:6-9)

Week One Scanning:

Day One: Scan Genesis 1-11

Week One Daily Readings:

- **Day Two: Creation & The Garden of Eden**
  (Genesis 1-2)

- **Day Three: The Fall of Man & The First Murder**
  (Genesis 3-4)

- **Day Four: The Family of Adam**
  (Genesis 5)

- **Day Five: The Flood Account**
  (Genesis 6-7)

- **Day Six: Noah's Deliverance & God's Promise**
  (Genesis 8-10)

- **Day Seven: The Tower of Babel**
  (Genesis 11)

Devotions for Younger Children:

- **Day One**: *The Story and The Song* (Introduction from Psalm 19 & Hebrews 1)

- **Day Two**: *The Beginning: A Perfect Home* (p. 18-27)

- **Day Three**: *The Terrible Lie* (p. 28-37)

- **Day Four**: Review the first two days. Have your child describe what creation might have been like. Do you think it looked different from the way the world looks today? Internet search "Adam and Eve Coloring Sheet" and download a picture for your child to color about creation.

- **Day Five**: *A New Beginning* (p. 38-47)

- **Day Six**: Review yesterday's reading. Have your child describe what it may have been like for Noah's family on the ark. What emotions did Noah's family experience? How did they feel being in the ark? Were there dinosaurs on the ark? Internet search "Noah's Ark Coloring Sheet" and download a picture for your child to color about the flood.

- **Day Seven**: *A Giant Staircase to Heaven* (p. 48-55)

Notes

Notes

Week Two Scanning:

- **Day One**: Scan Genesis 12-50

Week Two Daily Readings:

- **Day Two: God Covenants with Abraham**
  (Genesis 12-13, 15)

- **Day Three: The Sign of the Promise**
  (Genesis 17-18)

- **Day Four: Sodom & Gomorrah**
  (Genesis 19)

- **Day Five: Isaac**
  (Genesis 21-22, 24)

- **Day Six: Jacob & Deception**
  (Genesis 27-33)

- **Day Seven: Life of Joseph**
  (Genesis 37, 39-50)

Devotions for Younger Children:

- **Day One**: Review yesterday's reading, referring to the "Questions to Consider" on p. 65 for assistance.

- **Day Two**: *Son of Laughter* (p. 56-61)

- **Day Three**: Review yesterday's reading and reinforce Genesis 15:5 with the following activity:
    - Give your child one sheet of black construction paper. Then provide him/her with metallic star stickers. Have your child attach his/her stars to the black paper, leaving some space between them. Let your child use chalk/white crayon to connect and count the stars. Finish the picture by writing Genesis 15:5 at the bottom of the page.

- **Day Four**: Preview tomorrow's reading on the birth of Isaac with your child.
    - Gather some pictures from the day your child was born and describe how you felt in anticipation of his/her birth. Use this time to reinforce how special your child is, how loved he/she is, and how you view your child as a gift from God.

- **Day Five**: *The Present* (p. 62-69)

- **Day Six**: *The Girl No One Wanted* (p. 70-75)

- **Day Seven**: *The Forgiving Prince* (p. 76-83)

Notes

Notes

Week Three Scanning:

- Day One: Scan Exodus 1-20

Week Three Daily Readings:

- **Day Two: Israel's Suffering**
  (Exodus 1)

- **Day Three: Moses Becomes God's Instrument**
  (Exodus 2-4)

- **Day Four: Moses & Pharaoh**
  (Exodus 5-7:13)

- **Day Five: The Plagues**
  (Exodus 7:14 – Ch. 11, 12:29-30)

- **Day Six: The Passover & The Red Sea**
  (Exodus 12:28, 12:31 – Ch. 14)

- **Day Seven: God's Provision & The Ten Commandments**
  (Exodus 15-18, 20)

Devotions for Younger Children:

- **Day One**: Review yesterday's reading on Joseph. Ask your child about his/her thoughts concerning how Jacob showed favoritism towards Joseph. Was that good or bad? What did it make Joseph's brothers want to do? Was Joseph wrong for sharing his dreams with his brothers?

- **Day Two**: Read Romans 8:28. In what ways did this happen in Joseph's life? Take time to address a time when this verse applied to you or your family. If your family has gone through a tragedy, remind your child of the truth that God works together for good... according to His purpose.

- **Day Three**: *God to the Rescue* (p. 84)

- **Day Four**: Internet search "Ten Plagues Coloring Sheet" and download a picture for your child to color about the Ten Plagues in Egypt.

- **Day Five**: *God to the Rescue* (p. 85-91)

- **Day Six**: *God Makes a Way* (p. 92-99)

- **Day Seven**: *Ten Ways to Be Perfect* (p. 100-107)

Notes

Notes

Week Four Scanning:

- **Day One**: Scan Leviticus – Malachi

Week Four Daily Readings:

- **Day Two: Offerings Instituted**
  (Leviticus 1-7)

- **Day Three: The Israelites Enter the Promised Land**
  (Joshua 1-6)

- **Day Four: The First Earthly King of Israel**
  (1 Samuel 8-10, 14-15, 31)

- **Day Five: The Second Earthly King of Israel**
  (1 Samuel 16-20 & 2 Samuel 1-2, 5)

- **Day Six: The Wisdom of Solomon**
  (Any 3 chapters of Proverbs & Ecclesiastes 1-3)

- **Day Seven: The Promise of the Messiah**
  (Isaiah 7, 9, 11, 49, 52, 53)
    - Can you find them all and their New Testament fulfillment in Jesus?

Devotions for Younger Children:

- **Day One**: Identify the Ten Commandments in Exodus 20 with your child. Write them out on a piece of paper as you find them. Ask your child which one is the easiest to obey? Hardest? Which one does he/she wish was not included? Why? Put them on your refrigerator and commit to memorizing them over the next week.

- **Day Two**: *The Warrior Leader* (p. 108-115)

- **Day Three**: *The Teeny, Weenie…True King* (p. 116-117)

- **Day Four**: *The Teeny, Weenie…True King* (p. 118-121)

- **Day Five**: *The Young Hero and the Horrible Giant* (p. 122-129)

- **Day Six**: *The Good Shepherd* (p. 130-135)

- **Day Seven**: *Operation "No More Tears!"* (p. 144-151)

Notes

Notes

Week Five Scanning:

- **Day One**: Scan Matthew – John

Week Five Daily Readings:

- **Day Two: The Birth of Jesus**
  (Matthew 1-2 & Luke 2-3:22)

- **Day Three: Jesus Calls His Disciples**
  (Luke 5-6 & John 1)

- **Day Four: John the Baptist**
  (Luke 1, 3:23-38 & Matthew 3, 11, 14)

- **Day Five: Sermon on the Mount**
  (Matthew 5-7)

- **Day Six: Parables of Jesus**
  (Mark 4, 12-13)

- **Day Seven: Jesus Brings Healing**
  (Matthew 8-9 & Luke 7-9)

Devotions for Younger Children:

- **Day One**: *Get Ready* (p. 170-175) & *He's Here* (p. 176-183)

- **Day Two**: *The Light of the Whole World* (p. 184-191) & *The King of All Kings* (p. 192-199)

- **Day Three**: *Heaven Breaks Through* (p. 200-207)

- **Day Four**: *Let's Go* (p. 208-213)

- **Day Five**: *The Singer* (p. 228-235)

- **Day Six**: *Treasure Hunt* (p.250-255)

- **Day Seven**: *Washed With Tears* (p.280-285)

Notes

Notes

Week Six Scanning:

- **Day One**: Scan the last three chapters of each of the Gospels (last four of John) & Romans

Week Six Daily Readings:

- **Day Two: The Betrayal and Arrest**
  (Matthew 26, Mark 14, Luke 22, John 18)

- **Day Three: The Crucifixion**
  (Matthew 27, Mark 15, Luke 23, John 19)

- **Day Four: The Resurrection**
  (Matthew 28, Mark 16, Luke 24, John 20-21)

- **Day Five: The Promise Realized Through Faith in Jesus**
  (Romans 3-6)

- **Day Six: Righteousness Based on Faith in Jesus**
  (Romans 7-11)

- **Day Seven: Reconciled to God**
  (2 Corinthians 5, Ephesians 2:13-17, Colossians 1:15-20)

Devotions for Younger Children:

- **Day One**: *The Servant King* (p. 286-293)

- **Day Two**: *A Dark Night in the Garden* (p. 294-301)

- **Day Three**: *The Sun Stops Shining* (p. 302-309)

- **Day Four**: *God's Wonderful Surprise* (p. 310-317)

- **Day Five**: Review this week's readings, referring to the "Questions to Consider" on p. 65 for assistance.

- **Day Six**: *Going Home* (p. 318-325)

- **Day Seven**: Internet search "Heaven Coloring Sheet" and download a picture for your child to color. Discuss what you learned in your readings this week about how to get to heaven.

Notes

Notes

Week Seven Scanning:

- **Day One**: Scan Acts, Galatians – Colossians, & 2 Thessalonians – Jude

Week Seven Daily Readings:

- **Day Two: Promise of and Function of the Holy Spirit**
  (John 14 & Acts 1-2)

- **Day Three: Spiritual Gifts**
  (1 Corinthians 12, Ephesians 4:1-16, Romans 12:3-8)

- **Day Four: Peter's Boldness**
  (Acts 3-5, 10-12)

- **Day Five: Persecution of the Church**
  (Acts 6-8)

- **Day Six: Saul's Conversion**
  (Acts 9, 26:12-32, 1 Corinthians 9:1, 15:8)

- **Day Seven: The Church Spreads**
  (Acts 13-19)

Devotions for Younger Children:

- **Day One**: Internet search "The Apostle Paul Coloring Sheet" and download a picture for your child to color.

- **Day Two**: *God Sends Help* (p. 326-333)

- **Day Three**: Identify three of the seven spiritual gifts listed in Romans 12:6-8. Where do these spiritual gifts come from? Draw a picture of a scenario of someone using one of these gifts.

- **Day Four**: Internet search "Peter the Disciple Coloring Sheet" and download a picture for your child to color. Describe what you learned about Peter in your reading today to your children as he/she colors.

- **Day Five**: Go to **www.WorldWatchList.us** and view the 50 countries where persecution among Christians is highest. Watch the video "What can you do in 5 minutes with your child." Begin praying for countries where persecution is highest and take the 5-5-5 challenge.

- **Day Six**: *A New Way to See* (p.334-341)

- **Day Seven**: Internet Search "Church Coloring Sheet" and download a picture for your child to color. Describe what you learned about the spread of the church in your reading today to your child as they color.

Notes

Notes

Week Eight Scanning:

- Day One: Scan 1 Thessalonians & Revelation

Week Eight Daily Readings:

- **Day Two: Signs of Jesus' Return**
  (Matthew 24 & Joel 2)

- **Day Three: The People's Character**
  (2 Timothy 2-3 & 2 Peter 2-3)

- **Day Four: The Man of Lawlessness & The Beasts**
  (Daniel 7-8, 2 Thessalonians 2, 1 John 2:18-29, Revelation 12-13)

- **Day Five: Jesus Returns Again**
  (1 Thessalonians 1-5 & Revelation 22)

- **Day Six: The Marriage Supper of the Lamb & The Thousand Year Reign**
  (Revelation 19-20:6)

- **Day Seven: Satan Defeated & The New Heaven and New Earth**
  (Revelation 20:7-21)

Devotions for Younger Children:

- **Day One**: *A Dream of Heaven* (p. 342-349)

    Use household items to create the *Armor of God* this week with your child. You can find online crafts that will help you brainstorm how you put this together. Each day, explain the function of each part of the armor found in Ephesians 6:10-20. At the end of the week, discuss with your child how he/she will put on the *Armor of God* each day and why that is important. Reinforce each part's function. Take a picture of your creations and post them to Calvary's Facebook page.

- **Day Two**: *Belt of Truth* (Ephesians 6:14)

- **Day Three**: *Breastplate of Righteousness* (Ephesians 6:14)

- **Day Four**: *Gospel Shoes* (Ephesians 6:15)

- **Day Five**: *Shield of Faith* (Ephesians 6:16)

- **Day Six**: *Helmet of Salvation* (Ephesians 6:17)

- **Day Seven**: *Sword of the Spirit* (Ephesians 6:18)

Notes

Notes

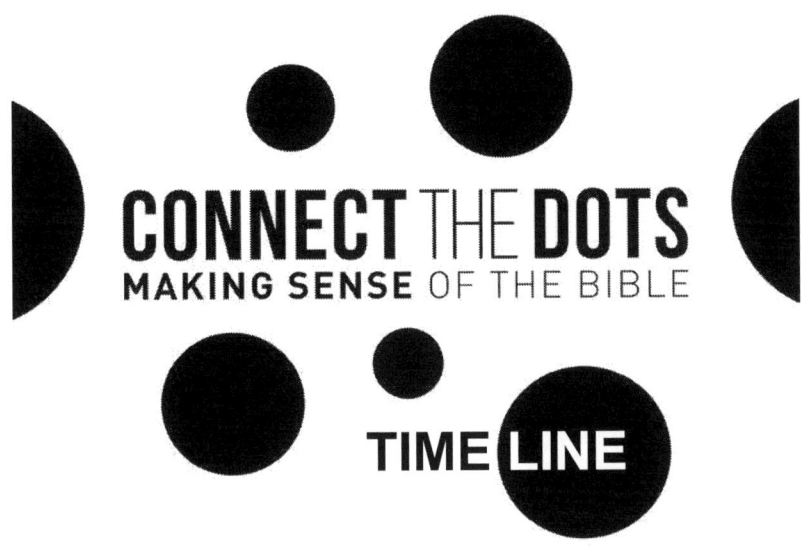

Old Testament
New Testament

     Triangular relationships are often used in psychotherapy to indicate the process by which two people (particularly in a family) in conflict, force a third party to choose sides. Identifying these types of relationships in the Bible accounts will help you connect the dots to their family situation and how it fits into the bigger picture of the Bible.
     Pick one of the triangular relationships on the next two pages and identify the two characters in conflict and the third being forced to choose sides. Use the Characters Index on pages 177-178 to help you find the biblical reference.

OLD TESTAMENT

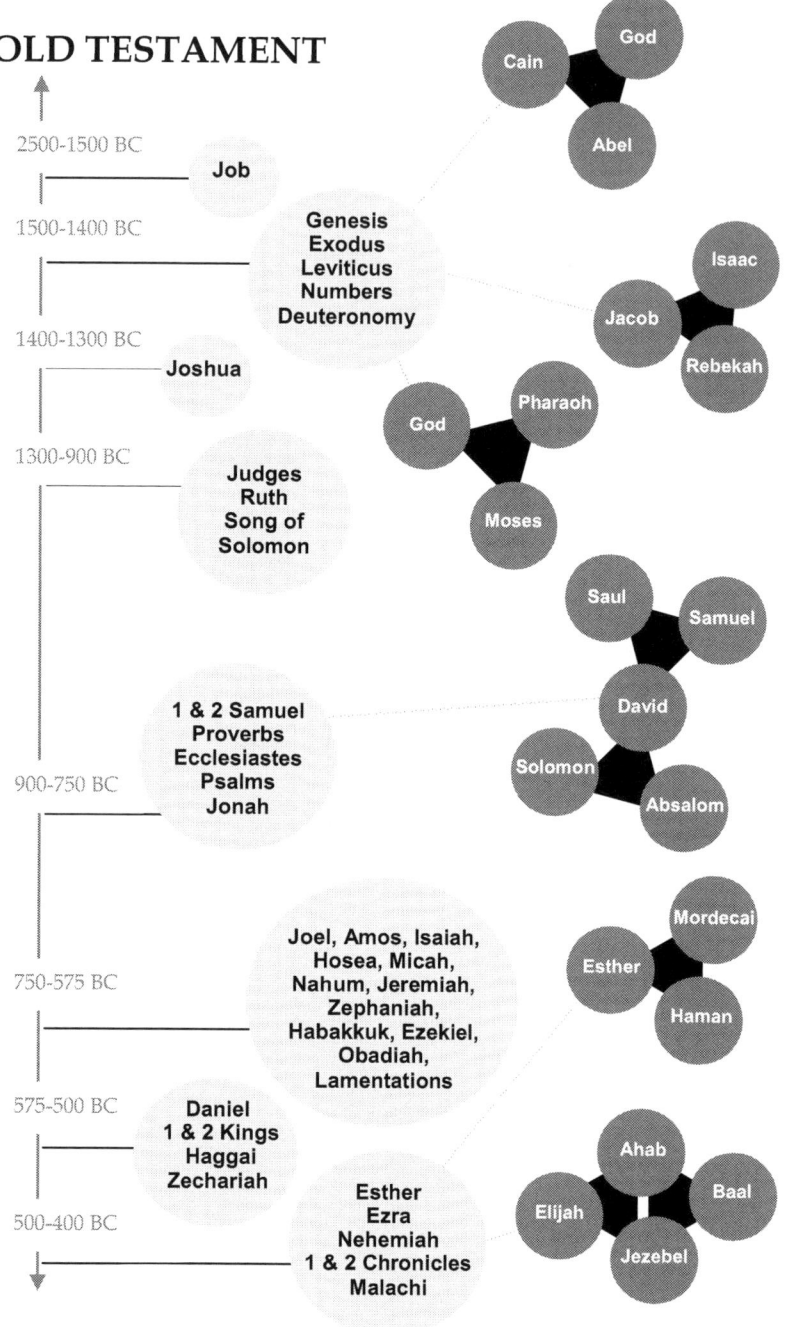

NEW TESTAMENT

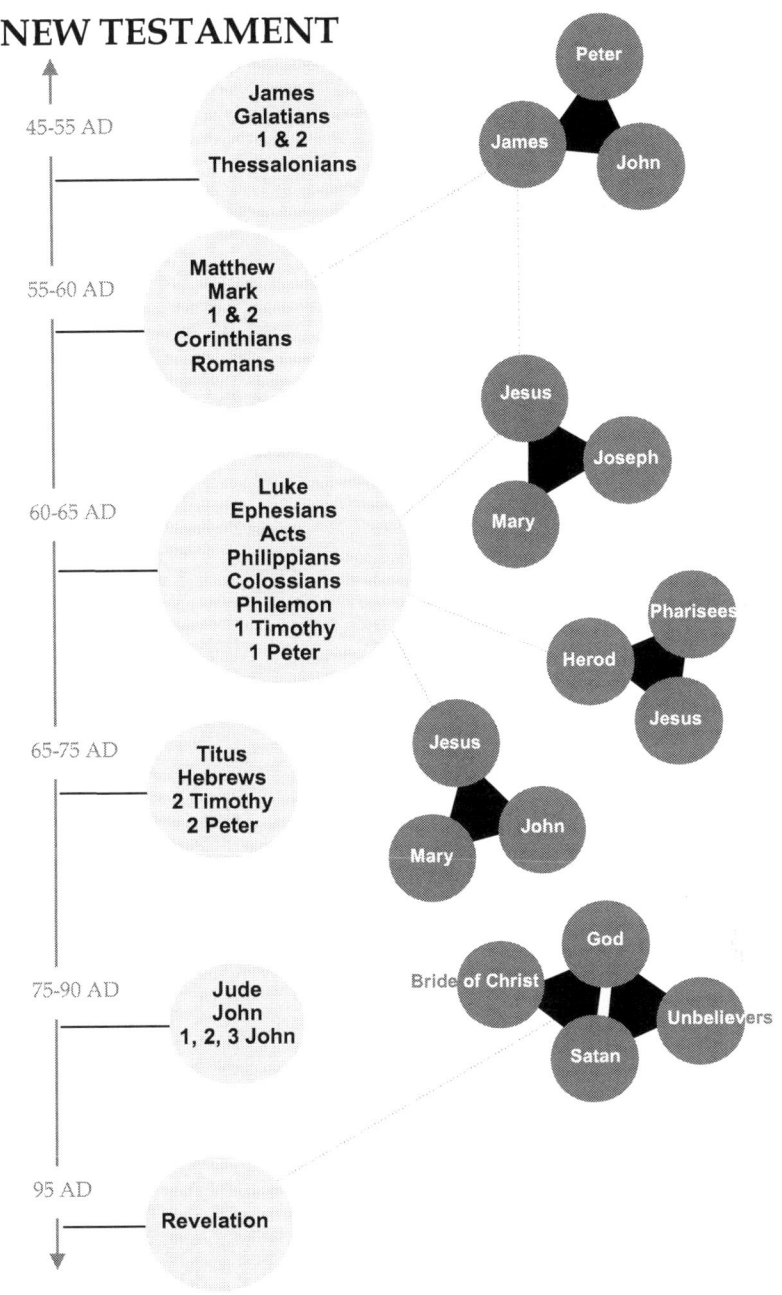

The List: 50 Characters in the Bible

Bonus List: The Dirty Dozen

Scripture

50 Characters in the Bible - Index

Aaron (*12*, 19, 20)
Abel (*12-13*, 55)
Abraham (*13-14*, 17, 23, 24, 42, 47)
Adam (*14*, 39, 55)
Barnabas (*15*)
Daniel (*15-16*, 28)
David (*16-17*, 24, 45-47, 52)
Elijah (*17-18*, 26, 41, 53, 58)
Elisabeth (*18*, 29)
Elisha (*18-19*, 58)
Esther (*19-20*, 36-37, 56)
Eve (*14*, 55, 63)
Ezra (*20-21*)
Gideon (*21*, 54)
Hezekiah (*22*, 24)
Isaac (13, 17, *23*, 24, 42)
Isaiah (22, *23-24*)
Issachar (*24*)
Jacob (17, 23, *24-25*, 30, 34, 42, 45)
James (*25-26*, 28-29, 41)
Jeremiah (*26*, 34)
Jesus (12-15 ,19, 24-32 , 34-36, 40-43, 47-48, 54, 57, 59, 61-63)
Job (*27-28*, 63)
John (13, 25, *28-29*, 41)
John the Baptist (19, *29-30*, 57)
Jonah (*30*)
Joseph (25, *30-31*, 37, 47)
Joseph, foster father of Jesus (*31-32*, 36)
Joshua (*32-33*)
Josiah (26, *33-34*)
Judah (*34*)
Lazarus (*34-35*)

Luke (*35*)
Mary Magdalene (*35-36*)
Mary, mother of Jesus (19, 24, 27, 31-32, *36*)
Mordecai (19-20, *36-37*, 56)
Moses (12, 22, 32-33, *37-38*, 41, 47, 60)
Nehemiah (20-21, *38-39*)
Noah (28, *39-40*)
Paul (15, 35, *40-41*, 47, 48, 61)
Peter (25, 29, *41-42*)
Rebekah (23, 24, *42*)
Ruth (*43*)
Samson (*43-44*)
Samuel (16, *44-45*, 46)
Saul, Son of Kish (16, 36, *45-46*)
Solomon (*46-47*)
Stephen (40, *47*)
Timothy (*48*)
Uzziah (*48*)

The Dirty Dozen - Index

Absalom (17, *52*)
Ahab (17-18, *53*, 58)
Baal (17, 33, 53, *54*, 58)
Cain (12-13, *55*)
Haman (20, 37, *56*)
Herod (26, 29, *57*)
Jezebel (18, 53, *58*)
Judas (25, 29, *59*)
Pharaoh (31, 37-38, *60*)
Pharisees (27, 47, 59, *61*)
Pilate (*62*)
Satan (14, 27, 28, 54, *63*)

Scripture – Index

Genesis 1:1 (p. 68)
Genesis 1:26-27 (p. 27)
Genesis 1:31 (p. 63)
Genesis 3:1-6 (p. 63)
Genesis 3:6 (p. 14)
Genesis 3:7 (p. 14)
Genesis 3:14-19 (p. 14)
Genesis 3:16 (p. 63)
Genesis 4 (p. 55,66)
Genesis 4:1 (p. 55)
Genesis 4:1-2,25 (p. 14)
Genesis 4:2 (p. 55)
Genesis 4:3 (p. 55)
Genesis 4:5-7 (p. 55)
Genesis 4:8 (p. 55)
Genesis 4:9-10 (p. 55)
Genesis 4:11-12 (p. 55)
Genesis 4:12, 14 (p. 55)
Genesis 4:13-14 (p. 55)
Genesis 4:15 (p. 55)
Genesis 5:4 (p. 14)
Genesis 6:5 (p. 39)
Genesis 6:7 (p. 39)
Genesis 6:8-21 (p. 39)
Genesis 6:22 (p. 39)
Genesis 7:1-12 (p. 39)
Genesis 8:15-9:17 (p. 39)
Genesis 15:5 (p. 145)
Genesis 17:17 (p. 13, 23)
Genesis 21:5 (p. 23)
Genesis 21:12 (p. 23)
Genesis 22 (p. 23)
Genesis 24:13-21 (p. 42)
Genesis 24:25 (p. 42)
Genesis 24:34-61 (p. 42)
Genesis 24:67 (p. 42)
Genesis 25:19-26 (p. 24)
Genesis 25:25-26 (p. 42)

Genesis 25:27-34 (p. 24)
Genesis 27 (p. 24)
Genesis 27:1-29 (p. 42)
Genesis 27:41-46 (p. 42)
Genesis 29-32 (p. 25)
Genesis 37 (p. 25)
Genesis 37:3 (p. 31)
Genesis 37:12-36 (p. 31)
Genesis 38 (p. 34)
Genesis 39-41 (p. 31)
Genesis 45:7 (p. 31)
Genesis 46:30 (p. 25)
Genesis 49:8 (p. 34)

Exodus 1 (p. 37)
Exodus 1-14 (p. 60)
Exodus 1:8-14 (p.60)
Exodus 1:15-16 (p. 60)
Exodus 1:17-22 (p. 60)
Exodus 2:1-10 (p. 37)
Exodus 2:11-25 (p.38)
Exodus 3:14 (p. 69)
Exodus 5:2 (p. 60)
Exodus 5:4-21 (p. 60)
Exodus 7-14 (p. 38)
Exodus 7:12 (p. 63)
Exodus 7:14-12:30 (p. 60)
Exodus 9:12 (p. 60)
Exodus 14:4 (p. 60)
Exodus 14:5-9 (p. 60)
Exodus 14:15-31 (p. 60)
Exodus 17:8-13 (p. 33)
Exodus 20 (p. 153)
Exodus 20:11 (p. 63)
Exodus 32:1-20 (p. 12)
Exodus 32:17 (p. 33)

Leviticus 10:1-2 (p.12)
Leviticus 19:2 (p. 70)

Numbers 13:8 (p. 32)
Numbers 14:19 (p. 71)
Numbers 14:28-30, 38 (p. 32)
Numbers 20:7-13 (p. 12)
Numbers 21:3 (p. 38)
Numbers 21:4-9 (p. 22)
Numbers 27:15-23 (p. 33)

Deuteronomy 4:3 (p. 54)
Deuteronomy 6:4-9 (p. 8)
Deuteronomy 6:5 (p. 72)
Deuteronomy 6:6-9 (p. 139)
Deuteronomy 22:20 (p. 36)
Deuteronomy 22:20-21 (p. 32)
Deuteronomy 34:10 (p. 38)

Joshua 11:17 (p. 54)
Joshua 24:15 (p. 73)
Joshua 24:31 (p. 33)

Judges 2:10-23 (p. 54)
Judges 2:12 (p. 74)
Judges 6 (p. 21)
Judges 8:33 (p. 54)
Judges 8:33-9:6 (p. 21)
Judges 13:3-7 (p. 43)
Judges 14:6, 19, 15:14, 16:28-29 (p. 44)
Judges 14:8-9 (p. 44)
Judges 16:1 (p. 44)
Judges 16:4-20 (p. 44)
Judges 16:17 (p. 44)
Judges 16:21 (p. 44)

Ruth 1:16 (p. 43, 75)
Ruth 2:1-23 (p. 43)
Ruth 3-4 (p. 43)
Ruth 3:10 (p. 43)

1 Samuel 2:18-19, 3:1-21 (p. 44)
1 Samuel 2:26-36 (p. 44)

1 Samuel 3:19 (p. 45)
1 Samuel 3:20 (p. 44)
1 Samuel 7:3-4 (p. 44)
1 Samuel 8:1-3 (p. 44)
1 Samuel 8:10-18 (p. 45)
1 Samuel 8-10 (p. 44)
1 Samuel 9:15-17 (p. 45)
1 Samuel 13:8-15 (p. 45)
1 Samuel 13:13-15 (p. 44)
1 Samuel 15 (p. 45)
1 Samuel 15:17 (p. 45)
1 Samuel 16 (p. 45)
1 Samuel 16:1-13 (p. 16)
1 Samuel 16:7 (p. 76)
1 Samuel 22:17-19 (p. 46)
1 Samuel 25 (p. 45)
1 Samuel 31 (p.46)

2 Samuel 6:2 (p. 54)
2 Samuel 7:11-16 (p. 16)
2 Samuel 7:18 (p. 77)
2 Samuel 11-12:25 (p. 17)
2 Samuel 13 (p. 51)
2 Samuel 13-19:8 (p. 51)
2 Samuel 14:25 (p. 51)
2 Samuel 15:6 (p. 51)
2 Samuel 16:22 (p. 52)
2 Samuel 18:1-19 (p. 52)

1 Kings 2:10-25 (p. 46)
1 Kings 3:16-28 (p. 46)
1 Kings 9:10-19 (p. 46)
1 Kings 11:26-40 (p. 47)
1 Kings 11:33 (p. 47)
1 Kings 16-21 (p. 58)
1 Kings 16:29-22:40 (p. 53)
1 Kings 16:30 (p. 53)
1 Kings 16:31 (p. 58)
1 Kings 16:32 (p. 53, 58)
1 Kings 16:33 (p. 53)

1 Kings 18:19 (p. 58)
1 Kings 18:20-40 (p. 17, 53)
1 Kings 18:20-19:2 (p. 58)
1 Kings 19:8 (p. 18)
1 Kings 19:11-12 (p. 78)
1 Kings 21:1-16 (p. 58)
1 Kings 21:17-22:40 (p. 53)
1 Kings 21:23 (p. 58)
1 Kings 21:25 (p. 53, 58)
1 Kings 22:39 (p. 53)

2 Kings 1:1-18 (p. 54)
2 Kings 1:8 (p. 29)
2 Kings 2:9-12 (p. 18)
2 Kings 2:15 (p. 18)
2 Kings 2:19-22 (p. 19)
2 Kings 2:23-24 (p. 19)
2 Kings 4:1-7 (p. 19)
2 Kings 4:8-37 (p. 19)
2 Kings 4:38-41 (p. 19)
2 Kings 6:5-7 (p. 19)
2 Kings 8:11-15 (p. 19)
2 Kings 9 (p. 58)
2 Kings 9:1-26 (p. 58)
2 Kings 9:30-37 (p. 58)
2 Kings 14:1-7 (p. 48)
2 Kings 14:25-27 (p. 30)
2 Kings 17:16 (p. 54)
2 Kings 18-19 (p. 22)
2 Kings 18:4 (p. 22)
2 Kings 20:19 (p. 22)
2 Kings 23:25 (p. 33, 79)

1 Chronicles 5:5 (p. 54)
1 Chronicles 9:35-36 (p. 54)
1 Chronicles 12:32 (p. 24)
1 Chronicles 28:9 (p. 80)

2 Chronicles 7:14 (p. 81)
2 Chronicles 24:20-22 (p. 66)

2 Chronicles 26:1-15 (p. 48)
2 Chronicles 26:16-23 (p. 48)
2 Chronicles 33:21-25 (p. 33)
2 Chronicles 34:1-7 (p. 33)
2 Chronicles 34:8-28 (p. 33)
2 Chronicles 35:20-25 (p. 34)

Ezra 7:10 (p. 20, 82)

Nehemiah 1:4-11 (p. 38)
Nehemiah 1:11 (p. 39, 83)
Nehemiah 4 (p. 38)
Nehemiah 5 (p. 39)
Nehemiah 6:15 (p. 39)
Nehemiah 8:1-3 (p. 21)
Nehemiah 8:8-12 (p. 21)

Esther 2:7 (p. 36)
Esther 2:10 (p. 20)
Esther 2:17 (p. 19)
Esther 2:18 (p. 36)
Esther 2:19-23 (p. 37)
Esther 3-7 (p. 56)
Esther 3:1 (p. 56)
Esther 3:2-5 (p. 56)
Esther 3:2-6 (p. 37)
Esther 3:6-11 (p. 56)
Esther 3:6-15 (p. 56)
Esther 3:7-15 (p. 37)
Esther 3:8-15 (p. 20)
Esther 3:9 (p. 56)
Esther 4:13-14 (p. 37)
Esther 4:14 (p. 20,84)
Esther 5-8 (p. 20)
Esther 5:1-8,7:1-2 (p. 56)
Esther 5:9-14 (p. 37)
Esther 5:10,14 (p. 56)
Esther 6:13 (p. 56)
Esther 7:1-10 (p. 37)
Esther 7:3-7 (p. 56)

Esther 7:10 (p. 56)
Esther 10:2 (p. 37)

Job 1-2 (p. 28)
Job 1:1 (p. 27)
Job 1:8, 2:1 (p. 63)
Job 3:1-26 (p. 28)
Job 4-11 (p. 28)
Job 37:14 (p. 85)
Job 38-41 (p. 28)
Job 42:10-17 (p. 28)

Psalm 19:14 (p. 86)

Proverbs 1:7 (p. 87)
Proverbs 16:18 (p. 22)

Ecclesiastes 3:1 (p. 88)

Song of Solomon 8:7 (p. 89)

Isaiah 6:8 (p. 23)
Isaiah 7:14 (p. 24, 32)
Isaiah 9:6 (p. 24)
Isaiah 14:12-15 (p. 63)
Isaiah 40:31 (p. 90)
Isaiah 53 (p. 24)

Jeremiah 1:2, 5 (p. 26)
Jeremiah 9:1 (p. 26)
Jeremiah 16:2 (p. 26)
Jeremiah 29:11 (p. 91)
Jeremiah 20:7-18 (p. 26)
Jeremiah 26:7-15 (p. 26)
Jeremiah 43:1-3 (p. 26)
Jeremiah 52:28-30 (p. 20)

Lamentations 3:22-23 (p. 92)

Ezekiel 28 (p. 63)

Ezekiel 28:12-13 (p. 63)
Ezekiel 36:27 (p. 93)

Daniel 1-2 (p. 16)
Daniel 3 (p. 16)
Daniel 4:25 (p. 94)
Daniel 6:22 (p. 16)

Hosea 2:16-17 (p. 54)
Hosea 6:6 (p. 95)
Hosea 9:10 (p. 54)

Joel 2:13 (p. 96)

Amos 5:6 (p. 97)

Obadiah 1:15 (p. 98)

Jonah 1:1-3 (p. 30)
Jonah 1:4-16 (p. 30)
Jonah 1:17-2:1 (p. 30)
Jonah 2:2 (p. 99)
Jonah 3:4-6 (p. 30)

Micah 6:8 (p. 100)

Nahum 1:7 (p. 101)

Habakkuk 2:20 (p. 102)

Zephaniah 3:17 (p. 103)

Haggai 2:7 (p. 104)

Zechariah 4:6 (p. 105)

Malachi 3:10 (p. 106)

Matthew 1:2-3 (p. 34)
Matthew 1:5 (p. 43)

Matthew 1:19 (p. 36)
Matthew 1:20-21 (p. 32)
Matthew 1:24-25 (p. 36)
Matthew 2:1-11 (p. 57)
Matthew 2:16-18 (p. 57)
Matthew 2, 14 (p. 57)
Matthew 3:3-17 (p. 29)
Matthew 3:4 (p. 29)
Matthew 4:1-11 (p. 63)
Matthew 4:6 (p. 63)
Matthew 4:21-22 (p. 28)
Matthew 10:3-5 (p. 59)
Matthew 11:2-3 (p. 29)
Matthew 11:11 (p. 30)
Matthew 12:46-47 (p. 36)
Matthew 13:36-43 (p. 27)
Matthew 13:55 (p. 36)
Matthew 14:1-12 (p. 57)
Matthew 16:16 (p. 41)
Matthew 17:1-8 (p. 25, 29, 41)
Matthew 23:1-4 (p. 61)
Matthew 23:5-36 (p. 61)
Matthew 23:35 (p. 13, 65)
Matthew 26:14-16 (p. 59)
Matthew 26:33-35,69-75 (p. 42)
Matthew 26:36-46 (p. 25, 29)
Matthew 27:3 (p. 59)
Matthew 27:3-4 (p. 59)
Matthew 27:5 (p. 59)
Matthew 27:6-10 (p. 59)
Matthew 27:15-23 (p. 62)
Matthew 27:24-26 (p. 62)
Matthew 27:57-61 (p. 62)
Matthew 28:19-20 (p. 110)

Mark 1:16 (p. 41)
Mark 1:17 (p. 111)
Mark 1:19 (p. 25)
Mark 1:21, 29-31 (p. 41)
Mark 1:35-42 (p. 41)

Mark 2:18 (p. 29)
Mark 3:6 (p. 61)
Mark 3:17 (p. 26)
Mark 3:20-22 (p. 54)
Mark 3:23-29 (p. 54)
Mark 6:14-29 (p. 29)
Mark 7:1-13 (p. 61)
Mark 10:35-45 (p. 26)
Mark 14:27-15:47 (p. 36)
Mark 15:2 (p. 62)
Mark 15:40 (p. 36)
Mark 15:47 (p. 36)
Mark 16:1-8 (p. 36)
Mark 16:9 (p. 36)

Luke 1:5-80 (p. 29)
Luke 1:6 (p. 18)
Luke 1:28 (p. 36)
Luke 1:37 (p. 18)
Luke 2:4-5 (p. 31)
Luke 2:7 (p. 112)
Luke 2:8-33 (p. 32)
Luke 2:35 (p. 36)
Luke 3:1 (p. 62)
Luke 3:3-17 (p. 29)
Luke 7:36-50 (p. 61)
Luke 8:49-56 (p. 25, 29)
Luke 9:54 (p. 26)
Luke 11:29-32 (p. 30)
Luke 13:1 (p. 62)
Luke 18:10-14 (p. 61)
Luke 20:46-47 (p. 61)
Luke 22:8 (p. 29)
Luke 22:21 (p.59)
Luke 22:31 (p. 63)
Luke 24:44 (p. 65)

John 1:1, 14 (p. 66)
John 1:44 (p. 41)
John 3:16 (p. 113)

John 4:23-24 (p. 55)
John 11:1-45 (p. 35)
John 12:5-6 (p. 59)
John 14:2-3 (p. 27)
John 14:25-26 (p. 107,108)
John 18:3 (p. 61)
John 18:28-19:16 (p. 62)
John 19:4 (p. 62)
John 19:26-27 (p. 36)
John 21 (p. 42)

Acts 1:8 (p. 114)
Acts 1:12-25 (p. 59)
Acts 1:18-19 (p. 59)
Acts 4:27 (p. 62)
Acts 4:36 (p. 15)
Acts 6:8 (p. 47)
Acts 6:10 (p. 47)
Acts 7:51 (p. 47)
Acts 7:54-60 (p. 47)
Acts 7:58 (p. 40, 108)
Acts 8:1 (p. 40)
Acts 9:26-27 (p. 15)
Acts 12:1-2 (p. 26)
Acts 13:22 (p. 17)
Acts 14:6-23 (p. 48)
Acts 15:36-41 (p. 15)
Acts 16:1-2 (p. 48)
Acts 18:3 (p. 40)
Acts 22:3 (p. 40)
Acts 22:4 (p. 40)
Acts 22:21-22 (p. 41)
Acts 23:1-10 (p. 61)

Romans 5:12-21 (p. 14)
Romans 6:23 (p. 27, 115)
Romans 8:28 (p. 149)
Romans 8:34 (p. 27)
Romans 10:9-11 (p. 27)
Romans 11:11-31 (p. 13)

Romans 12:6-8 (p. 165)
Romans 14:5 (p. 9)
Romans 15:4 (p. 7)

1 Corinthians 4:17 (p. 48)
1 Corinthians 10:31 (p. 116)

2 Corinthians 4:7 (p. 117)
2 Corinthians 5:10 (p. 27)
2 Corinthians 7:10 (p. 59)
2 Corinthians 11:3 (p. 14, 63)
2 Corinthians 11:14 (p. 63)

Galatians 5:22-23 (p. 118)

Ephesians 6:10-20 (p. 63, 169)
Ephesians 6:11 (p. 119)

Philippians 2:20-22 (p. 48)
Philippians 4:6 (p. 120)

Colossians 1:15-17 (p. 27)
Colossians 3:2 (p. 121)
Colossians 4:11-14 (p. 35)
Colossians 4:14 (p. 35)

1 Thessalonians 5:16-18 (p. 122)

2 Thessalonians 3:3 (p. 123)

1 Timothy 3:6 (p. 63)
1 Timothy 6:12 (p. 124)
1 Timothy 6:13 (p. 62)

2 Timothy 1:2, 7 (p. 48)
2 Timothy 1:5, 3:14-15 (p. 48)
2 Timothy 1:12 (p. 125)
2 Timothy 3:16-17 (p. 65, 66)
2 Timothy 4:9 (p. 48)
2 Timothy 4:11 (p. 35)

Titus 2:11-12 (p. 126)

Philemon 4 (p. 127)
Philemon 24 (p. 35)

Hebrews 2:14-15
Hebrews 10:23 (p. 128)
Hebrews 11:4 (p. 13, 55)
Hebrews 11:12 (p. 14)
Hebrews 11:32 (p. 44)
Hebrews 11:32-34 (p. 21)
Hebrews 11:37 (p. 26)
Hebrews 12:24 (p. 13)

James 1:27 (p. 129)
James 2:19 (p. 63)

1 Peter 3:15 (p. 66)
1 Peter 5:7 (p. 130)
1 Peter 5:8 (p. 63)

2 Peter 3:9 (p. 131)
2 Peter 3:15-16 (p. 107, 108)

1 John 1:9 (p. 132)
1 John 2:2 (p. 27)
1 John 4:14 (p. 27)

2 John 1:6 (p. 133)

3 John 1:11 (p. 134)

Jude 3 (p. 135)

Revelation 3:20 (p. 136)
Revelation 12:10 (p. 63)
Revelation 12:12-17 (p. 63)
Revelation 20 (p. 63)
Revelation 20:10 (p. 63)

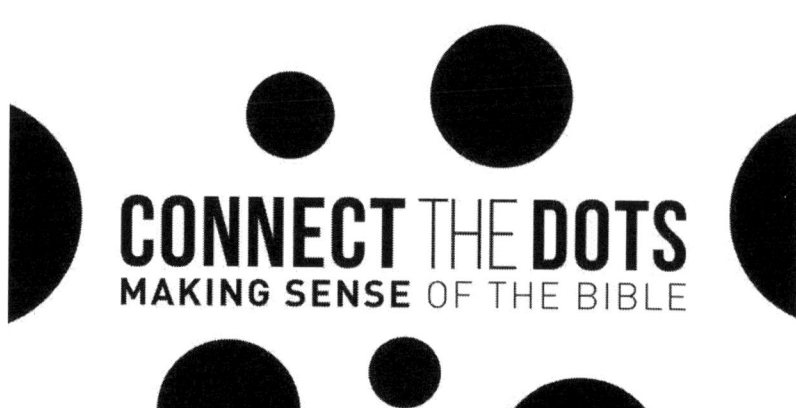

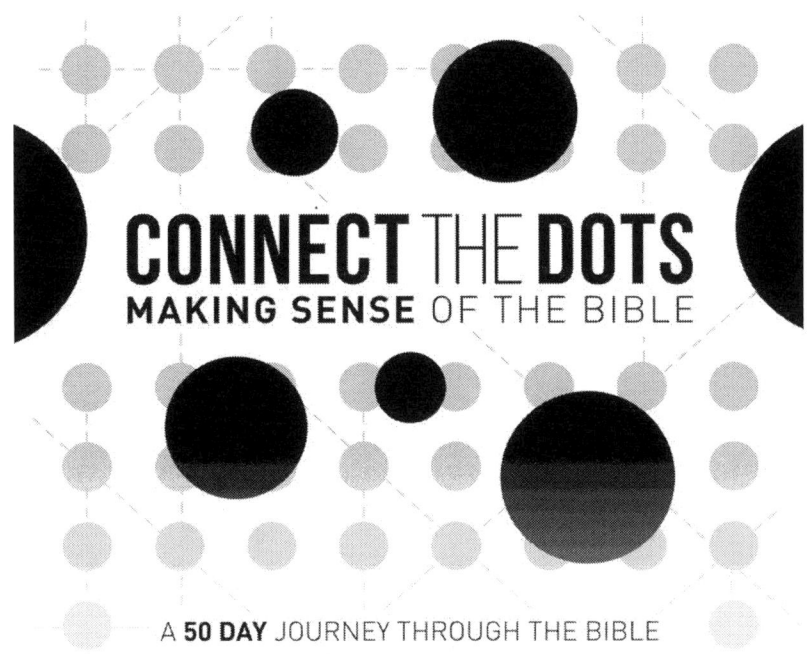

YOUR CHURCH. YOUR SMALL GROUP.
Nurture Authentic Community

A group is the best place to learn biblical truth and connect with other people. You can get lost in a large group, but in a smaller group you build real friendships, and you are able to discuss and learn spiritual truths from the Bible. Order the group study and get a group started at your home, work, or school and begin experiencing dynamic life in Christ today!

Nurture Authentic Community

Life has meaning and purpose that can only be found in God.
Willy Rice
Pastor, Calvary Church

www.Calvary.us/Curriculum

Other Resources from
CALVARY CHURCH, CLEARWATER

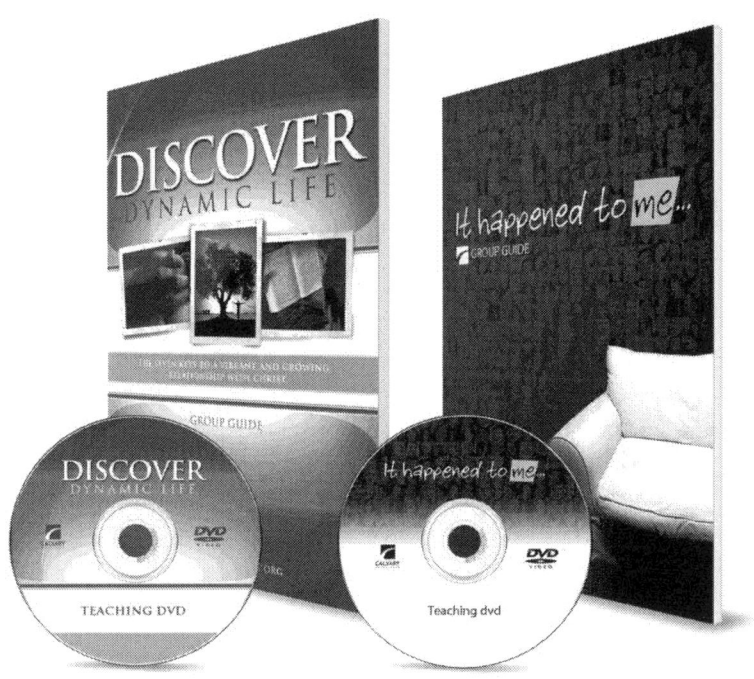

These two series come complete with a facilitator and participant guide along with a teaching DVD. A companion book to *Discover Dynamic Life*, written by Willy Rice, is also available. *Discover Dynamic Life* explores seven life-long habits that lead to dynamic life in Christ, while *It Happened to Me* includes the stories of seven people in scripture who modeled real faith.

www.Calvary.us/Curriculum

Made in the USA
Charleston, SC
13 January 2014